I WENT TO MOSCOW

Canon Stockwood outside St. Basil's Cathedral, Moscow

I WENT TO MOSCOW

BY

MERVYN STOCKWOOD

LONDON : THE EPWORTH PRESS

THE EPWORTH PRESS
(FRANK H. CUMBERS)
25-35 City Road, London, EC1

MELBOURNE   CAPETOWN
NEW YORK   TORONTO

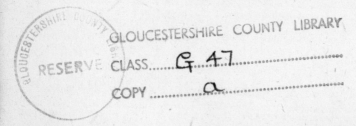
PRINTED BY PURNELL AND SONS LTD. PAULTON (SOMERSET) AND LONDON

IN MEMORY OF

RICHARD STAFFORD CRIPPS

*His Majesty's Ambassador in
Moscow 1940–42*

CONTENTS

LIST OF ILLUSTRATIONS

Chapter One

HOW I WENT TO MOSCOW

SINCE I came back from Russia the prejudice I have encountered has proved a formidable difficulty. On the one hand are the Communist sympathizers who identify the Soviet experiment with Heaven on earth, and on the other the double-dyed Blues who identify it with Hell let loose. After a public meeting at which I had spoken about my visit I heard a man say: 'Anybody can see the man is a Communist. It's true he made one or two criticisms of the régime, but that was only camouflage to sell the main idea. Like all Communists he is diabolically clever.' A few minutes later another person remarked to her friend: 'I always said he was a Tory through and through. I've never heard such reactionary stuff in my life—it was just one pack of lies.' In fact I am not a propagandist and I went to Russia with an open mind to see things for myself, not to prove anything. I have been interested in the Soviet Union ever since I was an undergraduate at Cambridge and I have studied Marxism and written about it. I have even ploughed through the massive tome *Soviet Communism—A New Civilization*, by the Webbs, a fact which drew from Sir Stafford Cripps the quip: 'It's good to know that at least three people have acquainted themselves with one thousand two hundred and sixteen pages of Soviet information—Mervyn Stockwood and Sidney and Beatrice Webb.'

But perhaps I had better tell the story of how I went to Russia because it will show that, so far from being a preordained Red or Blue plot, it was the result of a momentary inspiration, economically determined. In May 1953 I had an idea. I wanted to go abroad for my annual holiday, but I knew that, as a parson's pay permits no extras, I should have to work my passage. In previous years I had gone to Switzerland and earned my keep by acting as a chaplain. I had had some splendid times and I shall always retain happy memories of my temporary charges at the feet of the Jungfrau and the Matterhorn, and the glorious walks which culminated in luscious meals, washed down with good Swiss wines. I half thought of applying again for Zermatt, but I knew my friend Ronald R. Williams, now Bishop of Leicester, would be on the short list and, apart from the fact that he was a better candidate, he had more right to go because he genuinely climbs mountains with axes, hobnailed boots and the appropriate Alpine impedimenta, whereas I only walk in light shoes or sit on a chair-lift. Moreover, I wanted to see a country I had never visited before and have a complete break with my ordinary job. But that landed me in a difficulty. The only other string to my professional bow is occasional journalism, and I knew that an editor was unlikely to commission me to report on a continental holiday. And at that point I thought of Russia. I had always hoped to go there one day and I realized that I might find a newspaper to sponsor the trip, so I approached Dudley Barker, the features editor of the *Daily Herald*. He was enthusiastic, but stressed the difficulty of obtaining a visa. 'But supposing I manage to get a visa somehow, will the *Herald* sponsor me and foot the bill?' 'Probably yes, but how are you going to get the visa? All sorts of people have tried and failed.' 'I know, Dudley, but guileless parsons sometimes succeed where you wise boys fail.'

That evening I phoned Mr Attlee to enlist his support. I told him what was in my mind and explained that I thought it might interest the readers of the *Daily Herald* if I were to write a few straightforward objective accounts of people and things in the Soviet Union. I added that it was my intention to go as a private individual, sponsored neither by the Church nor by a political party. He wished me luck and said he would do all he could to help, but felt the Soviet authorities might not be keen to endorse a commendation from him. 'But I'll have a word with Harold Wilson tomorrow, as he is temporarily *persona grata* with them because he's recently been engaged in trade discussions.' He did, and a few days later Harold Wilson advised me to make a formal application to the Soviet Embassy, promising to send a covering note himself. I don't know how many strings he had to pull, but I am certain he worked hard on my behalf, writing letters and interviewing officials. I shall always be grateful to Harold Wilson; if it had not been for his generous efforts I should never have got my visa.

But several months were to pass before I had cleared the hurdles. I had stated in my application that it was necessary for me to leave England in the last week of July as I had to be back at work at the beginning of September. For weeks I heard nothing. Now and again I had encouraging messages from Harold urging me to be patient and to keep my fingers crossed. My holiday began and still I heard nothing—so I went to Exmoor and fished. Each morning I anxiously awaited the postman, but the mail was as unhelpful as the trout. August dawdled languidly and wetly. I moved to the Lakes and to the Isle of Man, but the Soviet Ambassador seemed to be suffering from lock-jaw. I accepted the facts regretfully but philosophically, cast thoughts of Russia from my mind and returned to Bristol. And then the miracle happened. One morning in early September a polite note from the Embassy informed me that the visa had been granted.

Now, indeed, I was on the spot. I am no more conscientious or hardworking than thousands of others in similar positions, but I knew I had been absent from my parish for five weeks and I had sharp twinges of conscience about downing tools just as the winter's work was beginning. I thought it over and decided I could *not* decently go and if it had not been for a curious combination of coincidences my visa would have remained unclaimed. The fact is, Robert Birley, the Headmaster of Eton, and Sir Walter Monckton, the Minister of Labour, persuaded me to change my mind. Robert Birley was preaching for me and staying at the vicarage. Walter Monckton was in Bristol on constituency business and, as is his custom, came to my church for Holy Communion. We forgathered for an aperitif and I told them the story. 'You don't mean to say you've turned the visa down?' said Robert Birley with the charm and firmness which has made him such a successful and effective headmaster. 'You can't refuse; you simply must go. It's a chance in a lifetime.' He was ably seconded by Walter Monckton, and everybody knows his powers of skilful persuasion! 'My dear Mervyn, I know the parish will miss you, but I am sure you have everything so well organized you could withdraw for three weeks without serious trouble. I really think you ought to go.' In view of such pressure what could I do but meekly assent? I'm afraid these personal revelations will disappoint the Blue critics who are convinced that I am a secret agent of the Communist Party, because while it is true the way was prepared by such dangerous Leftists as Clem Attlee and Harold Wilson, the matter was clinched by a headmaster of Eton and a Conservative Cabinet minister.

Having squared my conscience, I now had to square my ecclesiastical superiors to get the necessary leave of absence. I approached my Bishop, Dr Cockin. This is not the place to say all I should like to say about the Bishop of Bristol, but no priest could have a more understanding diocesan. I mentioned, *inter alia*, that if I remained in England I should be away from the parish for part of the time in any event as I was due to go to London for Convocation. 'In that case, I think you had better go to Russia, as you can probably do more for the Kingdom there than at Convocation,' replied Dr Cockin.

But another month had to pass before I was able to leave, because I discovered that in addition to my Soviet visa I required a transit visa for Czechoslovakia and that necessitated cables to Prague and two visits to the Embassy in London. In addition, formalities had to be settled with the Russians.

I cherish the memory of my meeting with the Soviet official. It was at his official residence in Kensington Gardens on a beautiful autumn morning in October. He received me with courtesy and asked me to explain why I wanted to go to his country. I almost despaired. Months ago he had had my letter of application in which I had set out my reasons. Worse followed. He told me that it might take some time to get the visa confirmed. Then of course there were transport difficulties and currency problems. I was plunged into gloom, and then decided I must play for high stakes. I told him frankly that I could not afford to delay; that I must go immediately; that I was anxious to improve the relationships between our two countries by reporting honestly and objectively on what I saw. 'Honestly—yes, honestly,' he repeated after me, and then took me to the waiting-room. Ten minutes later I was called back. The atmosphere was different. He was friendly, helpful and enthusiastic. 'I can give you your visa now, though I shall want you to send me some more photographs and we will phone the aeroplane company and the bank to get everything settled at once.' He was as good as his word and within a few minutes the whole thing was fixed. I was amazed, and appreciative. 'Thank you, sir, for your help. I am most grateful for your assistance and interest.' 'Yes, it has all been done in less than an hour. But that is not surprising; my country hates bureaucracy.'

One thing puzzled me about this visit. When talking to the official I sat opposite him at his desk. Immediately on my left was a radio which was tuned in to a screeching soprano, making conversation difficult. I wonder if it was only a radio —or did it conceal a ticker-machine to take down my remarks? Perhaps I am stupidly suspicious, but I learnt that other visa applicants encountered the radio. Moreover, I met several similar models with screeching sopranos in my hotel in Moscow. And I wonder if the change of atmosphere while I was in the Embassy waiting-room was due to the fact that the ticker had given a satisfactory account?

A formidable obstacle to travelling in the Soviet Union is the rate of exchange. The pound is worth at least forty roubles, but for reasons best known to the Russians the rate is fixed at ten. This means that the value of the pound is reduced to five shillings. For Communists, 'fellow-travellers' and dupes this does not matter because as members of a delegation their expenses are covered, but it matters a lot to the private traveller, for it will cost him fifteen pounds a day to live in Moscow. I was indeed fortunate as the *Daily Herald* footed the bill. Even so we had to argue with the British Treasury, and my allowance, though generous, did not permit extras and, of course, it set a severe limit to travelling. I wanted to visit Leningrad, Stalingrad and Kiev, but it was impossible because I should have needed a hundred pounds more than the Chancellor was prepared to grant. I can only hope that the post-Stalin Government will be more sensible; if it wants visitors it must agree to a reasonable rate of exchange. And here is a tip worth passing on. A reduction can be effected by putting oneself into the hands of 'Intourist' before the journey begins. I did this, and bought a book of vouchers which enabled me to live at a first-class hotel, and instead of paying the cashier, which would have been appallingly expensive, the waiter removed a voucher after each meal. The cost of the vouchers was six pounds a day. The difference

between that and the fifteen pounds mentioned above is due
to incidental expenses, especially transport, which was often
ten pounds a day. So if as a result of reading this book you
decide to visit Russia, as I hope you will, be sure to ask the
Soviet Embassy to tell you how you can get a book of vouchers
—it will reduce your expenses by half.

I was warned by Harold Wilson to have a look at my
wardrobe because English clothes are not suitable for Russian
winters. I took the precaution of consulting the Embassy
official, and he told me that an October day in Moscow is like
a cold January day in London. To be on the safe side I made
a hurried visit to the shops and bought a set of thick under-
clothes and socks, a scarf and a pair of stout shoes. Perhaps
I am a warm-blooded individual and have a natural resistance
to cold, for I didn't notice much difference between the
climate of Russia and England, except on the last night at the
airport when it was snowing. In any case I often walked
about the streets in a lounge suit without hat or coat, as did
the few other Englishmen I met. But it is only fair to add
that passers-by looked at us as if we were crazy and probably
attributed our comparative nakedness to wicked capitalist
exploitation.

And now I must come clean on one matter. Although I had
told the Soviet Embassy my journey was as a private individual
to obtain information for a series of articles in the *Daily
Herald*, I did not think to add that I should, of course, offer
my services as a priest to the English-speaking Embassies.
And perhaps the visa might have been refused if they had
known. Communist sympathizers rarely call on their embassies, as they view the diplomatic corps with grave suspicion
and the Soviet authorities certainly do not encourage the
practice, as they know that the visitor can find at his embassy
detailed information about conditions in Russia and, which
is even more dangerous, interpreters who do not hold the
party card. But I need hardly explain to readers that a priest

is always a priest no matter where he is, and if people need his ministrations he is automatically on duty. I wrote to the Archbishop of Canterbury for his permission to exercise my orders while I was in Russia. His Grace readily assented and Walter Monckton paved the way by advising the embassies in Prague and Moscow of my arrival.

I shall always be grateful for the opportunities which came my way as a result of this unofficial chaplaincy. Fortunately, since the death of Stalin, an English priest in Finland is allowed to travel to Moscow on a number of occasions each year, but there is no resident pastor, so I felt that I was able to be of some use. On Sundays I held three services at the American Embassy and my congregation consisted of diplomats from Britain, New Zealand, Australia, Canada, and America. In return I was accorded a welcome which was as generous as it was helpful. Everything was done to assist me and the information bureaus supplied me with a mass of facts and statistics which, even if I had been able to discover them from other sources, would have entailed hours of research. Even more valuable were the informal talks, parties and excursions which taught me much and took me to places which otherwise I would not have seen.

A word about the diplomatic community. It is sometimes thought, especially among my Labour Party friends, that a British Embassy consists of the most hopeless collection of stiff-shirted Tory die-hards and it is presumed that their reactionary outlook hinders, and perhaps makes impossible, a reasonable understanding between Great Britain and a Leftist country. It is true that in one or two isolated cases I encountered a mentality which had some points in common with this supposition. These were people who did not wish to be in Russia, loathed it, had no desire to understand it, were utterly ignorant of what was happening and longed to return to the sort of society they understood. But they were exceptions. The majority were highly intelligent, broad-minded, fair in their judgements and anxious to learn. Perhaps most of them do vote Conservative, but they certainly did not betray to me their political affiliations. They knew I was a Socialist, and they went out of their way to show me things which they thought would interest a person with my opinions and usually they were things which reflected credit on the Soviet Union. It is the job of an embassy to interpret the Government of their country to the Government to which they are accredited and vice versa. The British Embassies do their job with distinction; and in passing let me raise my hat to the representatives of the U.S.A. I dislike the foreign policy of the Republican Government and I think Mr Dulles is a disaster. I dislike equally the mad hostility of the Soviet Union toward our American friends. But the delegation in Moscow, led by Charles Bohlen, is doing a delicate job superbly well in an atmosphere of extreme provocation. I certainly do not envy the diplomats in Moscow, as they have a lonely life. It is virtually impossible for them to mix with the population and they have to be content with going to one another's parties. Until recently their movements were severely limited and they were followed by guards, but there has been an improvement since Stalin's death and most of the restrictions, together with the guards, have disappeared. Soldiers, however, are still at the gates and careful note is made of visitors. By the end of my stay we were on comparatively good terms and we managed to exchange smiles!

My reference to the Archbishop and the chaplaincy has taken me ahead of schedule and we must quickly return to England where I am still completing the final details of my tour. I was anxious to keep my visit secret as I was afraid there might be a last-minute hitch, or undue publicity might lead to the cancellation of my visa. Fortunately the date of my departure coincided with the autumn session of the Canterbury Convocation so I was expected to be in London. I spent the night at my club and left at five o'clock in the morning and nothing appeared in the Press until after I had arrived in Moscow.

The journey to Amsterdam was uneventful, and I found it difficult to realize I was about to penetrate the Iron Curtain. But the atmosphere quickly changed when I boarded the plane for Prague. It had a seating capacity for sixty but, apart from myself, there were only three passengers, and we did the trip without a spoken word.

Prague airport, at which we arrived on an exceptionally beautiful October afternoon, had an air of melancholy desolation. My fellow-travellers were, I imagine, 'fellow-travellers' because the officials quickly disposed of them and I was alone. I wandered through deserted halls and corridors before being summoned to the passport and customs office. I answered innumerable questions and filled in several forms. Everybody was polite but distant and I had the feeling I was a representative of a hostile régime. So imagine my relief when a car drew up flying a small Union Jack. I am not a jingoist. I do not take kindly to exhibitions of nationalistic emotion, and talks about King and Country have always made me squirm, but I hope I am a reasonable sort of patriot; and even if my love for England is not vocal, it exists, especially when I am in a foreign land. But never have I been more pleased to salute my country's flag than when I found myself for the first time on the other side of the Iron Curtain. Not only did it give me a sense of protection, but it stood for human values which are of infinite worth. An embassy official, Mr Whetstone, met me and whisked me off to the Alcron Hotel where I was to stay for the night. I was delighted with Prague. It is an enchanting city. I am not surprised that the Czech Ambassador in London sat me down at a table in his study to show me photographs and I only wish I had had time to see the many places of interest of which he told me with pride and enthusiasm.

In the evening I went to the British Embassy, an attractive

castle-like medieval building in the heart of the city, to celebrate Holy Communion and to dine with the Chargé d'Affaires, Mr John Beith. From him I learnt a good deal about internal domestic conditions and a summary of the events which led to the Communist Revolution. Apparently a few determined trade-union leaders paralysed industrial life and, with the help of a couple of Communist Cabinet ministers in a coalition Government, compelled President Benes to accede to their demands. It is incredible that a handful of men who know exactly what they want can determine the destiny of a country. Perhaps we of the West do not realize how delicate is the plant of democracy, and how easily it can be uprooted. If we are to safeguard our inheritance we must be vigilant. Communists achieve power through the apathy, not the conviction, of the masses. They would never have been successful in Czechoslovakia if the ordinary trade unionist had turned up to his branch meeting and voted into positions of responsibility men with democratic ideas. The trouble is, most of us are so idle and apathetic we are content to let other people do on our behalf the things we are too lazy to do ourselves, even when the other people are committed to destroying everything in which we believe. And how foolish it is to have coalitions with Communists who, because of their doctrines, are pledged to exterminate the other parties in the coalition. I do not like coalitions in our own country between Conservative and Labour, as the result is usually the lowest common denominator; but at least the parties can be trusted to observe the rules of the game. That is not the case with the Communists, however, because they do not believe in the game. Perhaps the experience of Czechoslovakia has served as an amber light to the Western democracies. If so, the sufferings of this gallant nation will not have been in vain.

My bill for bed and breakfast at the Alcron Hotel came to five-pounds, an exorbitant price, but I gladly admit that I have never had such superbly cooked bacon and eggs for breakfast. I arrived at the airport at six o'clock, to find my plane grounded by fog. The officials recognized me and suggested that I might like to pass the time at the airport cinema. It was a small comfortable building with well-upholstered seats. The audience numbered about twenty, a mixture of passengers, officials, and flying-officers. I must have seen a dozen propaganda films: we wandered round and round collective farms, built endless dams and witnessed the reactionary plots of saboteurs and the *bourgeoisie*. At eleven o'clock I told the attendant who was sitting next to me that I was an Englishman and found politics on the screen a trifle boring. She said she quite understood my point of view and immediately arranged with the operator to put on a Walt Disney cartoon for my benefit. In fact I am not a Disney fan, but it was such a relief to find I was not longer trapesing around a collective farm.

I took no further risks and as soon as the cartoon was finished I left for the restaurant, where I was joined by half a dozen officials and passengers. Within a few minutes we were hard at it. It was an exciting debate and it certainly could not have taken place in Russia. We spoke freely and frankly and, although I was a Daniel in the lions' den, my opponents listened attentively and fairly to what I had to say.

They asked me what I thought about the films.

'All right as far as they go,' I replied, 'but they don't prove anything. Every country, even Franco Spain, has its spot factory, farm and clinic, but they are not necessarily typical of the general conditions. Even in the England of Baldwin and Chamberlain, an England I loathed, we had our progressive employers who insisted on decent conditions for the workers. And for years our local authorities have been building decent schools and hospitals.'

'Perhaps so, but Czechoslovakia is now a workers' State, and our Government is running our country in the interests of all of us, whereas Britain is dominated by a ruling class of rich men and reactionaries.'

'The trouble with you is that you are the victims of catch-phrases. Your workers' paradise is as wide of the mark as is the proletarian hell we are supposed to have in England. I admit we have a Tory Government and I regret it, but to suggest that Sir Winston Churchill's Cabinet is reducing the country to misery and squalor is ridiculous. They may not like the Welfare State, but it is still there. We have our health and insurance schemes, which means that we can all receive medical attention and, if in need, the State will look after us.'

They knew nothing about the Welfare State so I tried to enlighten them. Unlike their opposite numbers in Russia, with whom I was to have several fierce arguments, they seemed to believe me.

Then we got on to wages and housing.

'But if what you say is true, why do so many people in England live in castles with an income of £100,000 per annum?'

'In the first place, most of our castles are ruins. If they aren't, they've probably been taken over by the Coal Board or else the owners, down-at-heel viscounts living in a dilapidated wing, conduct the proletariat through the State apartments at half-a-crown a time. But to be serious, I admit we have our class division, but so have you. And, as with you, there are wide differences in income scales.'

'The differences in Czechoslovakia are not nearly as great as in Britain. Nobody here gets £100,000 a year.'

'And I doubt if anybody does in England, but if it does happen the Exchequer will take away £95,000 in income tax to finance the welfare services.'

They gasped with astonishment. They knew little of British taxes, and nothing whatever of death duties.

'But,' they asked, 'do your people feel that their country

belongs to them, as we feel Czechoslovakia belongs to us, and that everybody matters?'

'There I think you have got something. I detest your Communist régime, and many of the things you've made yourselves believe are bunkum and eyewash, but I admit you have a sense of purpose and responsibility which is, alas, lacking in Britain.'

Two hours quickly passed. We argued furiously, but neither side lost its temper and, as the Czech sense of humour is as good as the English, we laughed a lot. The fog cleared and they walked with me to the exit door. We shook hands and exchanged greetings. 'Goodbye, comrade, *bourgeois* priest, British friend, good journey, happy time in Moscow, and be sure to talk with us again when you return. We shall be waiting for you.' They did, and we had another round with the gloves off three weeks later when, appearing in the restaurant, I sat on a high stool at the bar and called to them: 'Come on, Bolshies, the capitalist parson is waiting for you to convert him.' I shall remember those meetings with pleasure. I respect those Czechs for their loyalty to their ideals, their courtesy and friendliness toward me and their genuine desire to be of service to their fellow men. One remark especially I pass on for consideration. It was made by a man in his early thirties: 'I am a Communist, but I am also a Catholic, and I still go to Mass every Sunday. I joined the Party because it was doing many of the things which the Church ought to have done years ago, but didn't do.'

The Russian plane was less comfortable than the ones to which I had been accustomed; it was like the converted service planes in which I had travelled to Switzerland immediately after the war. But it was adequate. We had a hostess, but she was silent and formidable and she did not speak to foreigners. We did not strap ourselves in as the plane took off, nor were we given barley-sugar to suck. Although there was no cooked meal neatly arranged on a tray, each passenger received a picnic carton containing dreary sandwiches and withered apples. It was sufficient to keep the wolf from the door, but, as I prefer to fast rather than munch unappetizing food, I made little impression on the carton. The Russians are curious people. They are so keen on propaganda, but when it comes to the simplest things they fail abysmally. If I wanted to convince a visitor of the superiority of the Communist way of doing things, I should not neglect cuisine. First impressions are important and attractive hostesses and tempting meals are a good investment. But, no doubt, my reactions are middle-class and *bourgeois* and altogether out of place in a proletarian paradise.

We touched down at Warsaw where, after a longish wait, we were joined by two dozen passengers, most of them Russians. I slept for the rest of the journey and did not become fully conscious until we were warned we were nearing our destination. It was an odd and almost indescribable sensation. For years I had heard and read about Moscow; in fact the very name had spelt the disruption of one way of living and the emergence of another which, for good or ill, had affected all countries and all peoples. And now, as I looked through the window of the cabin, I saw beneath me the myriad lights of this vast city shining through the night. Even more impressive was the glow of the red stars on the Kremlin, mere pin-points, but so expressively symbolic. And I thought of another star—not red, but white—which centuries earlier had led wise men to the manger of the Prince of Peace.

Moscow airport is impressive and very large. We must have taken ten minutes to reach the point of disembarkation after landing. Soldiers boarded the plane and took our passports and we were led to a spacious and comfortable waiting-room decorated with life-size portraits of Stalin. How tired I was to become of these dreary portraits. An Englishman can tolerate the faces of his rulers for a brief spell at a coronation

25

or a general election, but he intensely dislikes the thought of them guarding his waking and watching his sleeping. Moreover, most of the portraits and busts of Stalin are artistic abominations and reflect no credit upon Soviet painters and sculptors. It's time they grew up and took art seriously.

An Intourist guide, in a long black coat and slouch hat, introduced himself and conducted me to the customs officials, who afforded me an intensely interesting half-hour. Cigarettes, valuables and clothes received no attention, but I had to produce books, magazines, papers, and manuscripts. The first to be taken was my Bible. I said to the inspector I preferred him to leave it alone and he at once courteously returned it to its place. He then laid hold of four books and retired with them to a desk. There were H. A. L. Fisher's *History of Europe*, Arthur Bryant's *King Charles II*, Anthony Trollope's *The Last Chronicle of Barset*, and a manuscript book of sermons. The first three were disposed of fairly quickly, but the last had them foxed. The explanation was, of course, quite simple. Before leaving England I decided I would not use valuable time in Moscow writing sermons for the embassies, so I took with me a few addresses I had recently preached. The official read it and summoned a colleague. He was equally nonplussed, so both went with the book to an imposing gentleman in a green uniform with lots of gold braid. He read it. I turned to my guide and said: 'This is a compliment I value. As soon as I arrive in your atheistic country, I am responsible for three of your bosses acquainting themselves with the Gospel.' I don't think my quip was altogether appreciated.

It was nearly midnight as the taxi took me at top speed through the streets of Moscow. I was tired but so interested I eagerly watched everything. Two nights previously I had been in London, the night before in Prague, and now in Moscow, and all three seemed much the same. People leaving theatres, waiting for buses, going into restaurants, hurrying home, chatting on street corners. Political systems may differ, but human beings change but little.

We pulled up at the National Hotel which was to be my headquarters for the next few weeks. It is in the centre of the city and used to be a favourite haunt of the aristocracy. It is adequately comfortable, but its decorations and amenities suggest the Ritz in the reign of Queen Victoria. I was given a suite of rooms on the third floor—bedroom, sitting-room, and bathroom. I disliked them because they were appallingly noisy. The din in the Moscow streets at night is difficult to describe. There is constant coming and going and motorists never tire of tooting their hideously high-pitched horns. If a Communist high-up reads this book I hope he will pass on my criticism to the appropriate authority. Silence in the streets at night may be a *bourgeois* habit, but it's good for the nervous system and encourages sleep and even the workers' paradise might benefit from less cacophony.

In spite of the late hour the restaurant was full. The menu was printed in four languages which was a help, but the dishes, and there was an attractively wide assortment, were strange. I tried to discuss their potentialities with the waiter, but as he understood neither English nor French our conversation was not conspicuously coherent. But a Russian trade unionist who was dining with a delegation at a neighbouring table overheard us and he quickly came to the rescue. Incidentally that was typical of Russian courtesy. I often found myself in a fix but people invariably helped me out of my difficulties with infinite patience and kindliness. I have nothing but praise for my dealings with them. I have never found so much graciousness in any country, and I have not a single disagreeable memory.

Of course I broke my fast with caviare. How delicious it is! I never tired of it, although I had it three times a day. I do not usually eat breakfast, but while I was in the Soviet Union

my passion for the roe of the sturgeon overcame my prejudices. Then followed a beef-steak. I shall have more to say
about Russian cuisine later, but on this occasion I was well
content.

And so to bed.

Chapter Two

KALEIDOSCOPE

THE noise and the heat of the room woke me early, so I got up soon after daybreak and looked out of my window. The National Hotel is ideally situated for a tourist. If it were London and not Moscow, it would be in Whitehall within sight of the Houses of Parliament and Westminster Abbey. I had a splendid view of the Kremlin, Red Square, and the central underground station.

As I watched the people hurrying to work, and it was reminiscent of Piccadilly Circus, I was impressed by the width and cleanliness of the streets. They are a credit to any country, and might serve as an example to Great Britain. Apparently wholesale demolition was necessary to achieve such broad thoroughfares and in many cases rows of buildings have been set back several yards. The procedure was explained to me but, lacking a technical mind, I did not grasp the whys and wherefores. I was shown the square in which the City Council House is set and I was told that the entire area was moved on rollers. In the middle of the roads are two parallel lines and the track between them is reserved for the cars of V.I.P.s. I often saw large black limousines leaving the Kremlin and racing at tremendous speed along this holy ground. The police would blow their whistles and the rest of the world would get out of harm's way as quickly as possible. I tried hard to look into the cars as they flashed by, but it was useless as curtains were always drawn across the windows. How differently we do things in England. A few months back in a traffic jam in Oxford Street was the Prime Minister. He sat in his car, complete with boiler suit, sombrero and cigar, dictating letters to his secretary. It will be a happy day for Russia when its leaders can do the same.

But it must not be supposed that all the roads in the Soviet Union are like the main streets of Moscow. Far from it. There's many a narrow alley in the city and outside there's often no road at all, but only mud or rubble tracks. Once when I managed to leave my guide behind me I went for a longish motor-ride into the country. It was not without interest as the surface varied from macadam to earth and flint. But the authorities are making efforts to overhaul the transport system. It is a colossal undertaking and will take years and years to achieve. I saw large gangs of road-makers and menders, men and women, busily at work with spades and pneumatic drills. I was told they were prisoners and by their appearance I should think it likely. But, providing the conditions of labour are reasonably humane, it strikes me as a sensible arrangement. It is said that English prisons are over-full; perhaps the waiting list would be less heavy if the inmates were given arduous constructional jobs. Incidentally I asked my guides about Russian prisons and concentration camps, but they did not seem anxious to enlighten me, except to say there were no concentration camps in the Soviet Union. Perhaps it is a difference of vocabulary, because what they described as centres of re-education and culture would demand a more primitive definition in English! In any case, when I was visiting a transit camp in Germany and had the opportunity to talk with dozens of refugees and escaped prisoners, I learnt more than enough about Stalin's penal system. It is not as bad as Hitler's and it is probably no worse than General Franco's, but the West will continue to treat with reserve Russian claims of justice and enlightenment so long as there is reason to suppose that prisoners are not given a fair deal. At the same time it is true that certain types of domestic defaulters are wisely and humanely treated and trouble is taken to fit them into society. But there is a difference between domestic and political prisoners, just as there is a difference between the way the British treat desperadoes at home and in the colonies.

As we have got on to prisons, we might as well go a stage farther and look at political trials. I asked several questions about Beria, who was still alive. I said that although I had no love for the man I imagined he would make the usual forced confession and be shot. This caused furious indignation and I was told that Soviet justice prevented forced confessions and that Beria was guilty of trying to reintroduce the capitalist system with the help, of course, of the U.S.A. I continued the argument:

'It's all very well for you to say there are no forced confessions. That's what your Communist friends in Britain asserted a year ago when the seven doctors publicly repented of their crimes. In fact, in a debate with the Communists, I was described as a fascist for daring to dismiss the confessions as a tissue of humbug and lies. And then within ten days I was justified by what your own Government admitted.'

'Yes, but that was an exception and it was the work of Beria and assassins like him.'

'Maybe, but you cannot deny that your Mr Beria was in control for a very long time and, what he did once, he probably did on scores of occasions. To be frank, most of us in the West believe that the great trials and purges in 1936 were nothing more than cold-blooded murder, a particularly disgusting travesty of justice.'

'That's because you believe the lies of the capitalist Press. We know these men were the enemies of our country and were hoping to reintroduce capitalism.'

'My friends, I refuse to get angry, but you must remember you are talking to an educated man and not writing an editorial for the *Daily Worker*. You cannot expect me to believe that devoted pioneers who had sacrificed their lives for the

Communist cause would court execution by destroying what they had built up. One or two, yes; but not dozens. Human nature doesn't behave like that.'

Perhaps I should add that such frank expressions of opinion were reserved for my last days in Moscow! Even so I was listened to with politeness and shown the tolerance which is usually accorded to the invincibly ignorant. But the discussions lacked the spontaneity of the Communists at Prague. I felt I was listening to a gramophone record and I knew the answers before they were phrased. I am sure I made no impression whatever. It's odd how readily men will surrender their minds to an authority which is supposed to be infallible. The fact is, once the Soviet Government has spoken, the oracle is unquestionably accepted by the devotees. One oracle may contradict another, but for the converted there is no limit to the possibilities of mental gymnastics.

After looking at the roads I made my way to the restaurant for breakfast, where I had my first lesson in Russian patience. We complain in England about dilatoriness in eating-shops, but the most tortoise-like waiter is a sprinter when compared with his Russian counterpart. I waited ten minutes before being handed a menu. I did not mean to study it because I knew what I wanted: caviare and tea. But the man disappeared immediately and did not return for a quarter of an hour. I examined the cutlery and wine glasses—a curious collection which remained on the tables for all meals—and read two chapters of Trollope. I gave my order and tackled another twenty pages. The food arrived. It was good and well served.

I am a tolerably patient individual, but I hate wasting time and I like my day to run with the precision of a BBC programme. I quickly realized that I was to be faced with a major irritation throughout my visit and that I should have to accept philosophically the fact that punctuality means as little to the Russians as it does to the Irish—and that's saying a lot! I did what I could to expedite matters by taking my complaint to the head waiter. He was charming and I eventually ordered and ate a two-course meal in three quarters of an hour, which is just about half an hour longer than I usually spend. Although I could have had an extra course, I avoided it because I could not afford the expenditure of time.

I had not been in Moscow long before I found myself in difficulty with the food. That was not the fault of the National Hotel, but my own bad luck. As a child I had colitis, so I tend to have a weak stomach and rich food usually upsets me. And Russian food *is* rich. On my first day I had goose; on the second I tried, for the first time in my life, sucking-pig. Both were delicious, but for the next week I lived on toast, grapes, and small portions of caviare. When I had recovered I re-explored the menu and toyed with small portions of sturgeon, salmon, and turkey. Incidentally I managed to remain up except for one day when I had to take to bed. My guide was anxious to send for a doctor. I was about to concur when I realized that foreigners have to pay for medical attention and, the rate of exchange being what it is, that can be expensive; so I took the opportunity of pointing out that, thanks to Nye Bevan, visitors to England are treated as the guests of the country, but, as this custom had not reached the Soviet Union, I had better nurse myself. But the management could not have been more considerate. I was moved to a larger and quieter suite of rooms and afforded every comfort and for the rest of my stay there were constant inquiries about my health and no effort was spared to give me the right diet. Such courtesy was typical of my hosts and is one of my many delightful memories of the Soviet Union.

Now for something less pleasing. After a time I decided to eat privately in my rooms instead of in the restaurant. The change was not due to any hope of speeding up the meals: on the contrary it was, if anything, worse. I would ring the bell and wait and ring, and re-ring. In fact I reckoned that

c

33

I had to allow an hour to elapse from the first ring to the last mouthful. No, I left the restaurant because my squeamish stomach was not helped by the sight of Muscovites being sick at neighbouring tables. I am not suggesting that it happened regularly, but it did occur three times within two days. I am not a teetotaller, but I loathe the vulgarity of drunkenness. Even people who take a more tolerant view would not be best pleased to walk into an hotel like the Dorchester or the Savoy and find their fellow diners publicly disgracing themselves.

It is odd that the Government is not stricter. I saw more drunkenness in three weeks in Moscow than in my eighteen years in East Bristol. One Sunday evening I went to a smart restaurant with some friends where a dance was in progress. We counted seventeen men hopelessly intoxicated and making a nuisance of themselves. Part of the trouble is the cheapness of vodka. I found it most disagreeable on the few occasions I drank it. I felt as though I was consuming liquid fire. But apparently it takes a quick hold of people and, as it only costs sixpence a glass, its victims are numerous. There are no licensing hours and vodka is bought at all times of the day at kiosks and in shops. Champagne is popular too. I noticed in several large stores counters where one could buy a glass for a shilling. And very good it was. I had no idea that shopping could become such a pleasure. But it cannot be in the interests of any country for drink to have such a hold on the people because the repercussions must be serious. No doubt it's only a minority, but the minority is sufficiently large for the police to have sobering-up stations in many parts of the city. The Communist Party is opposed to insobriety and reference is made to its evil effects in its propaganda, but the Government is inclined to turn a blind eye. Religion is regarded by Marxists as opium, a drug which turns men's minds from the realities of life and encourages them to live in a Cloud-cuckoo land. I should have thought vodka to be a more serious rival —but perhaps that is the prejudice of a *bourgeois* priest!

Very different is the attitude of the authorities toward sex. I have already explained the difficulty I had at the airport with books, journals, and newspapers. The reason for the close inspection was not solely the fear of political heresy, but the supposition, not unfounded, that Western journalism is apt to be sordid. Russian papers are not allowed to mention sexual offences and the sort of pictures we take for granted in British magazines are unknown there. They told me in no uncertain terms what they thought of our papers and I wish I could mention the adjectives they applied to one of our Sunday papers. Of course they think the exploitation of sex is due to the evil machinations of the capitalist Press barons. The people must be kept quiet, and as religion has lost its hold, pornography is a substitute. In fairness I am bound to admit that Russian papers are appallingly dull. Although I belong to the minority which is interested in politics and economics, there is a limit to the amount of propaganda I can consume. In fact I am as reluctant to be confronted by collective farms, dams and Stakhanovites as I peruse the paper over my morning coffee as I am to see them on the screen when I go to the pictures. Nevertheless I am sure the Soviet Press policy is basically right and never was I more certain of this than when I returned to London and found nearly every paper headlining a particularly offensive case of sexual perversion. I am told by friends in Fleet Street that unless there is a generous dose of filth a paper will not sell. If that is so, the sooner the paper goes bankrupt the better. But I do not believe it. The politics of the *Daily Express* and its Sunday counterpart are anathema to me and I am sure Lord Beaverbrook will have an extra long sojourn in purgatory, but they have proved, all honour to them, that a paper can be popular without being pornographic.

Another pleasant omission in Moscow is the vulgar postcard. I hope I am reasonably broad-minded, but I cannot understand why we permit the sale of coarse postcards which

are not even funny. It's easy to talk about the prostitution of
Soviet art, but I would prefer a dreary card of Stalin, or even
a collective farm, to some of the cards I am sent from British
seaside resorts by well-meaning friends.

I am in no position to pass judgement on Soviet morals and
in any case I am inclined to believe that human beings are
much the same the world over, but I must speak as I find
and, the fact is, I never saw a prostitute on the streets of
Moscow. I thought my clerical collar might have been responsible for my favourable impression, though it is certainly
no protection in London where prostitution becomes more
blatant each year, so I consulted the embassies. They were
of the same opinion. Prostitution is virtually non-existent. I
am not assuming that men who are determined to satisfy their
lower natures will not find ways and means, but they cannot
parade their desires publicly. I asked my guide to what he
attributed the elimination of prostitution. He said that as all
women had to do a job of work there was no need to earn a
living on the street. Moreover, if anybody should try, drastic
action is taken by the police—presumably a rest at a centre of
re-education and culture. It's a pity we do not learn from the
Soviets. London is a disgrace and I often wonder what
foreigners think of us. It's about time the Government took
a tougher line. Instead of a nominal fine, prostitutes should
be placed in homes and given the chance to win their way
back into useful employment and citizenship. And sentences
of life imprisonment should be passed on pimps who treat
prostitution as a commercial racket. Furthermore the police
would be doing a greater service to the State if they spent
less time searching for minor motoring offences, and more
time cleaning up the streets. I have often argued the point
with policemen and I am invariably told that nothing can be
done. Since going to Moscow I refuse to believe it. My one
regret is that an atheistic Government has been successful
where a Christian Government has failed.

But in some respects the Soviets have carried their purity campaign too far. I was astonished to discover that innocent love-making is forbidden in public places. For years I have organized expeditions and picnics for the young people in my parish and I automatically presume that, during the course of the evening, most of them will pair off and walk hand in hand and, when the scenery lends itself, have a kiss or two. And why not? But if they did that in Russia, a policeman would blow a whistle and there would be trouble. For instance, one lunch hour I saw a factory worker meet his girl friend in a little park near a main road. Unfortunately a policeman on point duty could see them, and they had to wait for a bus to intercept the vision of the law before they could express their natural feelings. Puritanism rarely achieves its objective; instead it turns us into humbugs because we profess one thing and practise another. Oliver Cromwell may have been a political necessity, but he was a moral disaster and it took the extravagances of Charles II to help us back to sanity. Human nature cannot be suppressed, but it can be sympathetically directed. If we can give young people a positive set of values, we need not trouble them with a negative string of prohibitions. And if a boy gets too amorous, kindly leg-pulling will achieve more than a policeman's whistle. I loathe Puritanism in every shape and I shall always regard the self-righteous industrialists of the nineteenth century, with their alleged passion for the ten commandments and their ugly exploitation of their workers, as among the blackest villains in our country's history.

Perhaps the Russians are strict today because of their experience in the early days of the Revolution. While we can ignore the stupid stories of sexual licence which the opponents of the régime circulated and believed, 'bourgeois morality', which includes the marriage vow, suffered an eclipse. In fact the situation deteriorated sufficiently for Lenin to make a severe attack on promiscuity. And it did not take long for the

Soviet Government to see the red light. Whereas divorce used to be cheap and easy, it is now expensive and difficult and, although it is still permissible, it is discouraged. In fact I got the impression that the family unit is more jealously safeguarded than in England. My guides often told me that no country can hope to prosper unless its family life is sound. With that I whole-heartedly agree, and I could wish that Britain would be as realistic in its approach to the problem. I do not believe that divorce is always wrong, in fact in exceptional circumstances I have advocated it, but I am sure that the speed with which we make, unmake and remake marriages must have disastrous social consequences.

When we come to morality and manners in the wider sense, I was favourably impressed. The people may not be more honest basically, but as the penalties are more severe, they are careful not to put themselves on the wrong side of the law. If a man steals or, to use contemporary jargon which dislikes calling a spade a spade, 'scrounges', he is unlikely to be dismissed by the judge with a pi-jaw and a trifling fine. More probably will it mean a short vacation at a centre of re-education and culture, plus a little road-making. In the schools the need to be honest in speech and action is emphasized. Of course the approach is different from ours. We base our behaviour on moral principles and tell people to do the right because it is right. Marxist morality is pragmatic. Society cannot function properly if its members do not trust one another; hence a good comrade must be truthful and dependable. I do not think pragmatism is sufficient, but at least it is a beginning.

Russians are more polite than Englishmen—not that that would be difficult. On my last day in London I took a taxi from Paddington to my club in Pall Mall. Although the driver gave me no help with my cases, I gave him a ninepenny tip. He neither thanked me nor wished me good-day; instead he looked at the coins with contempt and scowled. And that is not the first time I have suffered from the boorishness of ill-mannered clods. Decent behaviour is, thank God, still found at all levels of society, but courtesy is no longer a national perquisite. Too often it is regarded as an unnecessary affectation or a badge of servility. Kindliness and gentleness are virtues which pour oil on the wheels of life, and I hope we shall be more insistent to teach this in our schools and practise it at our jobs and in our homes. The scoffers might well go to the Soviet Union and see for themselves what happens when a nation is naturally courteous.

I have already mentioned the kindliness of my guides and the hotel officials, but it was apparent everywhere. When I travelled in the Metro I noticed how boys and girls automatically gave up their seats to older people; when I was in the shops the attendants, instead of adopting the English 'take it or leave it' attitude, seemed anxious to please; when I went to the schools, clinics, churches and art galleries the people were obviously thoughtful toward one another. One night I got lost at the Bolshoi theatre. The ballet was due to begin within a few minutes, but as I had no guide with me, I mistook the entrance. There was an immense crowd in the vestibule and it was getting perilously near to the time the curtain was due to rise and, once that has happened, nobody is admitted until the end of the first act as late-comers are not tolerated. How I wish we had the same rule in English theatres! A Russian soldier, noticing my embarrassment, seized hold of me and took me with his party into a box which had been reserved for members of his regiment. In the interval he looked at my ticket and conducted me to my seat.

Here's another example. On my last day my guide asked me if I would like somebody to accompany me to the airport. As I was leaving at one o'clock in the morning, I declined. But he would not take no for an answer. 'It would be ungracious to let you leave our country without somebody to see you off.' The sceptic will, of course, attribute his concern for my welfare to security reasons, but that was not so. A special car and driver were chartered to take me from my hotel, the hotel officials were to see me into the taxi and the Intourist agency was to meet me at the airport. In any case, a man who could speak English appeared soon after midnight. He helped me with my luggage, talked merrily in the taxi, took me to the restaurant at the airport for a bowl of soup, and supplied me with magazines and sweets.

I am not pretending the Russians are saints, nor do I forget their appalling incompetence and dilatoriness which, apart from anything else, is a social nuisance; but I do contend that, by and large, the Muscovite is better mannered than the Londoner and that the rudeness, vulgarity and gracelessness which thrives in democratic Britain is less apparent in authoritarian Russia, where people seem to enjoy being agreeable to one another. To what extent the improvement is due to imposed discipline it is difficult to assess. Mr Attlee has recently complained about the litter that disfigures our countryside. In Russia the Government does not complain; instead it takes drastic action against the barbarians who throw paper and orange peel on the streets and that, no doubt, is why the streets and stations in Moscow are the cleanest in the world. Again, road accidents are caused partly by unavoidable accidents and partly by discourteous selfishness. I am given to understand that casualties are surprisingly small in Moscow as compared with London. I am not surprised. A car driver is allowed to commit three offences during his life. If he exceeds the maximum, he may never drive again; and the careless pedestrian receives similar treatment. We crossed the roads at given points. If we transgressed, a policeman descended upon us and demanded our papers. I nearly found myself in trouble several times, but the authorities, realizing I was a foreigner, took pity on me. The trouble was, the streets are so wide that I could never gauge whether I could get across before the lights changed. It was rather a terrifying experience. For instance, I would be in the midst of the famous Gorky Street when suddenly a fleet of cars would start to move, all sounding their hideous horns. I just stayed where I was and trusted to luck I would not be knocked down. When the avalanche had passed, I would smile at the policeman and pass on.

I never ceased to be surprised at the meekness with which the population accepted the prohibitions of their rulers. I would set out to a library or a museum and find it closed. As an Englishman I wanted to know why and complained bitterly at the inconvenience. My guide, however, seemed unruffled and invariably remarked: 'These things happen.' Once I defied the prohibitions and won. Toward the end of my stay, I decided to go out after dinner by myself and wander in the back streets. I walked several miles in the unfashionable parts of Moscow, tramping along alleys, walking into court-yards, and peering, whenever possible, through windows to study housing conditions. I got back to the centre of the city at midnight to find a large-scale rehearsal for the November parade in operation. The streets were cordoned off and I, like everybody else, was refused admittance. I tried various detours but all were useless, so I made a frontal attack on Gorky Street, because I knew that if I did not succeed I should not get back to the National Hotel for hours. Two soldiers intercepted me and refused to let me pass. I talked quietly and persistently to them in English; they replied in Russian. The uncomprehensible conversation continued, I never flagging for an instant. An officer arrived. I politely repeated the word 'British' about twenty times and he signed me on. When I raised my hat to him, he seemed pleased and saluted.

Soldiers remind me of uniforms. There was a plethora of them. The Russians are incurably ritualistic and with the ceremonial of the Tsarist court abolished and the grandeur of the Orthodox Church somewhat eclipsed, the Soviet régime has had to find its own outlets. I have no objection to ritual, colour and uniforms. As I have already said, I detest Puritanism which robs life of its gaiety and dignity and I have no sympathy whatever with my Labour friends who complain about coronations, Lord Mayors' shows and civic receptions. Just as I like sitting in Eton chapel and watching the boys walk down the aisle in their tail coats, watching a workers' demonstration on May Day with their jolly banners, being a guest at a Cambridge feast and eating delicious food in a hall lit by candles and drinking from a loving-cup, or taking part in the glorious and moving pageantry of a Midnight Mass at Christmas, so I am prepared to accept the synthetic ceremonial of the Marxist paradise. Even so, there should be a limit and my one complaint about Moscow is that, having removed the Tsar from his trappings, too many people have assumed them. London is great fun at a coronation, but three weeks are about as much as an Englishman can bear of fancy dresses. After that we begin to sigh for lounge suits and carpet slippers. But in Russia uniforms seem to be endless. I met them in streets, theatres, undergrounds, churches and libraries: all very splendid but there was a surfeit of them. All the same I did quite well out of it. In England I do not always wear a clerical collar, but I made up my mind that during my stay in Russia I would always use my badge of office as I did not wish there to be any misunderstanding. But I had not realized that the significance of a clerical collar would not be fully appreciated in the Soviet Union. The Orthodox priests have never worn them, nor have the Protestants, and as for the Roman Catholics, they are almost non-existent. So when I went to the ballet, especially when I was taken to the regimental box, my collar was assumed to be a top-ranking military decoration. And when I was introduced as *Canon* Stockwood it helped to convince my friends that I was a distinguished member of the artillery. I saw no reason to object to the deference accorded to me.

And what of the people themselves? How did they look?
What did they wear? I am glad I have been asked those
questions so frequently as it is human interests rather than
political ideologies which will help us to bridge the international gulfs. I never tired of looking out of my sitting-
room window at the crowds milling in the streets beneath
and when I went for walks the passers-by fascinated me. On
the whole they struck me as much the same as their contemporaries in any large European city. The younger generation
was vigorous, attractive, and often laughing. The older, a
trifle tired and bearing signs on its face of two devastating
wars. There was not the least suggestion of a sense of fear
or persecution; in fact, I am quite sure it does not occur to
the average Russian that he is living under a repressive dictatorship. He has never known anything but an authoritarian
régime and he does not sigh for the things he has never had.
When I was asked by my guide whether I would like to live
in Moscow permanently, I replied: 'Not until I can stand
outside the Kremlin on a soap box and tell whatever Government happens to be in power to go to hell—which is precisely
what we can do in England to our heart's content.' He was
amused and surprised and then I realized I was speaking of
something which was completely alien and unknown to the
Russian tradition. They know, of course, there are certain
things that must be left alone and not criticized, but it has
always been like that.

From the foreigners' point of view it is unfortunate that
these cheery, friendly people are not allowed to have any
dealings with them, unless authorized by the Ministry of
Foreign Affairs. Even then the meetings are never private or
personal, but in an office with several people present. I
repeatedly asked my guide to take me to a home so that I
could spend an evening with a family, but he said it was impossible. As I could not speak the language, I did not attempt
to enter into conversation with my neighbours at the ballet

or the theatre, but the experience of other people known to me suggests that it is prohibited. The Russian will give a short polite reply to an innocuous question and move away immediately. I saw that happen.

The Muscovite crowd is not smart. Clothes are adequate but badly cut, and the Russian physique is substantial rather than elegant. The men spoil their appearance with ill-fitting caps and uncleaned shoes. Although we probably do not realize it, there has been a revolution in working-class clothes in Britain since the war. When I began my ministry in Bristol in the days of unemployment, the men of my mission district wore ugly blue suits, white mufflers around their necks, and cloth caps. That has gone. Today, when they return from the factory, they change into quietly smart suits or, more often, sports coat and grey flannels. There has been a remarkable levelling of classes in this respect. So far as appearances are concerned, the different sections of society are almost indistinguishable from one another. No doubt the emphasis on consumer goods will soon make a similarly happy impression on Russia. Already felt hats are to be seen and there is a likelihood they will eventually oust the cap. Sports coats and flannels are not apparent, but the authorities have told the designers to study Western fashions, so perhaps they will come. I hope so, because the Muscovites look drab. The position will improve further when there is a more liberal allowance of boot polish and elbow grease. No matter how well dressed a man may be, he looks dowdy if his shoes are dirty.

During my first days I was on the look-out for security police about whom we have heard so much. I saw several and they seemed kindly, cheerful folk, especially the ones who accompanied me around the Kremlin. But, apart from that one incident, they didn't seem interested in my existence. Nevertheless I am sure foreigners, though not followed in the streets, are carefully watched. On every floor in the hotel a *grande dame* presided at a bureau and an obvious check was made on my movements. And the servants who cleaned my rooms seemed to take an unnecessarily long time tidying up my papers. On two occasions my brief-case, which I kept locked, was opened and letters arriving from the embassies seemed to suffer from a deficiency of gum, because the envelopes were usually unstuck. Whether or not there were microphones in my room I cannot say, though I do know several have been found at different embassies and, like other foreigners, I always went into the street when I wanted to have a private conversation. But let's be fair. On the day I arrived back in Britain I read in the evening paper that a question had been asked in Parliament about letters addressed to members of the Communist Party in Bristol being opened by the police. I myself suffered similar treatment at one stage during the war; but on this occasion the police had foolishly returned the wrong letter to the wrong envelope. So the British pot must be careful what it says about the Russian kettle when it comes to snooping.

Chapter Three

THE YOUNG IDEA

YEARS ago I was a schoolmaster and when I changed my profession I continued to hover on a beakish circumference. And from time to time I take part in the political scraps on the methods of education. Shall we get an educated democracy *via* the comprehensive school, or should we preserve the tripartite system and the eleven-plus examination? For these reasons I was particularly anxious to discover all I could about children in the Soviet Union. There is no doubt that in so far as there is a privileged class in Russia it consists of the youth of the country. I readily admit that much has been accomplished in Britain since the turn of the century, but we have not tackled the educational problem with the grit and determination of the Communists. They have treated it as we treat a major military operation. Money and men have been lavished upon it and there is a nation-wide strategy.

First, I went to a nursery where I saw a hundred and twenty babies. There was nothing spectacular about it as it was housed in an old building which used to belong to an affluent merchant. I was told there were dozens like it in all the Moscow suburbs. The director and the doctor, both women, welcomed me and immediately gave me a white coat. The staff consisted of eighty persons. I saw about ten, but I found it difficult to distinguish between nurses, supervisors and domestic helps. I liked the atmosphere of the place. It was jolly, friendly and inviting and the staff seemed really fond of the youngsters, who were healthy, robust and beautifully clean. Of course I wondered if it was a carefully prepared 'act' to impress me, but I am inclined to think that everybody was too busy to bother overmuch about a foreigner.

Some of the children were boarders, returning home for weekends, but the majority came for the day. I saw the babies in their cots and I noted their toys which were suspended in such a way as to encourage the exercise of muscles. The next age-group were crawling around in pens with more toys to stimulate movement. The three-year-olds who had been sleeping on the veranda were playing a musical game in a gaily decorated room. Their toys were on the large size, the idea being to encourage community effort and to prevent a child from sitting in a corner by itself.

These nurseries are not compulsory and, in spite of the extravagant claims, I think only a small proportion of children go to them, though there would be more if accommodation were less restricted. I have visited nurseries in England and the standard is about the same. The difference lies in the attitude of the authorities. We believe a child should stay at home with its mother unless there is special reason for her going to work. But the Soviet Government, with its insistence upon the parity of the sexes, encourages women to go with their husbands to the factory. I argued the point with the director by stressing the virtues of parental responsibility, but I was told that the desire to 'imprison a woman in her home' was a *bourgeois* superstition. Perhaps economics, rather than politics, is the determining factor. Housing conditions in Moscow are so bad that there is little incentive for a woman to stay indoors. Most working-class families are confined to one room and the daily chores can be done in a short time. So, if the mother does not go to work, she has to twiddle her fingers in a stuffy over-crowded room. Naturally she prefers to get away to the comparatively spacious atmosphere of the factory and leave her children at a nursery where the conditions are good. Moreover, although she and her husband have to pay about ten per cent of their joint income to the nursery, she will be able to supplement the family income and perhaps put something by for better living quarters, because in spite of official propaganda, decent accommodation is occupied by people who can pay for it.

Sooner or later a conflict will arise between the attitude toward family stability and the attitude toward sex equality. In the early days of the Revolution the family unit suffered an eclipse and the emphasis was placed upon the collective upbringing of children. This was not as bad as some Western critics made out. Just as wealthy parents in Britain entrust their young to nannies and private boarding-schools on the assumption that the development of character is helped by an early release from mother's apron strings, so the Communists believe that the Soviet State should make itself directly responsible for moulding its future citizens. And as the Soviet virtues were not fully appreciated, importance was attached to the educational possibilities of nurseries, kindergartens and schools. Those of us who work in industrial cities should have sympathy with this viewpoint. Although we talk a deal of hypocrisy about the sanctity of family life we know that many delinquents, spivs and gangsters would be decent citizens if only we had the power to remove them at an early age from bad parental influences.

But that does not alter the fact that ultimately a wholesome society must be built upon a wholesome domestic foundation. And the Soviets are wise enough to appreciate this. Hence the stress upon the home and the training of parents. No longer is divorce the device of a progressive socialist country to emancipate women. Marriage is a solemn contract which must not be broken except for special reasons after everything else has failed; in fact divorce is almost a disgrace which is grudgingly conceded by a disapproving State. And I suspect that when the need for female labour in the factories and on the farms diminishes, we shall hear less about sex equality and more about the glories of mothercraft and home-building.

*The Red Square: The Kremlin and St. Basil's Cathedral (now a museum)
and the mausoleum of Lenin and Stalin*

Cleaning a Moscow street in the early morning

Mozhaisk Highway, the main artery in the Kiev District of the capital

Before we leave the nursery, mention must be made of the arrangements for sending the children away for the summer vacations. The Government and the trade unions have a chain of sanatoria, rest homes and holiday camps for workers, parents and children. They are not compulsory but they are a regular and popular feature of Soviet life and are increasingly used. If necessary they are free, but usually the parents pay thirty per cent of the cost. I haven't a shadow of doubt we should be wise to follow the Russian example. Many a family would surmount their domestic rocks if holiday homes were provided for dispirited and tired mothers and for children who have nowhere for play but the streets. So far we have only toyed with the problem. It is time that the Government, the schools, the trade unions and the doctors put their heads together and formulated a policy.

My guide was anxious that I should visit a kindergarten. He spoke enthusiastically about it and seemed to imagine we had nothing like it in the West. In fact it is a version of our infants' school, the difference being that in Britain all children must go whereas in Russia attendance is not obligatory.

The child leaves the nursery for the kindergarten at three and remains there until seven when compulsory education begins. The kindergarten I saw was in a fairly prosperous suburb in two smallish houses which had been knocked into one. There were a hundred and fifteen children and a staff of twenty-three. Sixty-five of the youngsters were weekly boarders which is one of the reasons for the large staff, as allowances have to be made for night duty. The teaching staff gets a weekly wage of £3 15s. per week, and the domestic staff £2 15s. The day began with physical exercises at 8.45, followed by breakfast; studies and games until noon; lunch at 1; rest period and outdoor activities until tea at 4; studies until 7; supper and bed.

The school was clean and the children well turned out. The doctor had a room in the building and she kept a close watch on medical records. I asked to be taken to the kitchens and found the cook preparing the lunch. Everything was spick and span and the food looked and smelt most inviting. Here is the menu for the day of my visit: *Breakfast*. Egg, bread and butter, caviare; *Lunch*. Soup, rissole and potatoes, grapes; *Tea*. Cake and tea; *Supper*. Rice pudding, bread and butter, glass of milk. I thought the arrangements were better than those which prevail in our schools. Not only was the home-cooked food an improvement on the tepid hodge-podge which comes in containers from central kitchens, but there was a special dining-room with small gaily decorated tables and, what is more, children were taught table manners. It is an odd thing that in England we allow our children to eat anyhow, whereas in Russia there is an insistence upon the conventionalities and decencies usually associated with the middle classes.

The toilet arrangements were not up to ours. The washing basins and baths were adequate, but they would have been none the worse for a polish. The lavatories were not good, but that is not surprising as the standard throughout the country is lamentable. It is difficult to understand why a Government which shouts incessantly about hygiene and puts white coats on visitors on every conceivable occasion should tolerate disgusting lavatories. If, gentle reader, you are thinking of visiting the Soviet Union, as I hope you are, take my advice and abjure public conveniences and, if you will pardon my kindly intentioned bluntness, be sure to put a toilet roll or two in your valise. Harold Wilson gave me this last piece of advice and never have I had more cause to be grateful to a politician. Perhaps the new look of the post-Stalin era will become apparent in Soviet plumbing. If so, let him start with the schools and then rebuild every public convenience throughout the entire country. It will cost money, but I imagine the comrades will live longer and public expenditure on dysentery will diminish.

My guide spoke much about musical appreciation and he thought I should be surprised and enthralled by the Soviet approach to music in junior schools. I wasn't. Actually I love music, but there is a time and place for everything. I often think there is too much singing in our British schools and the children would be better employed learning to read and write. It was the same at this kindergarten. I sat through song after song, watched musical games, and listened to percussion bands—which I hate—until my head reeled and I asked to be taken to the handicrafts department. By all means let there be some, but enough is as good as a feast. Mind you, when the child moves on to the senior school it's a different story. There he gets a thorough grounding in the classics, which is why Russia is the most musically cultivated nation in the world. All honour to her for that, and may the West follow her example.

The handicrafts room, which was liberally decorated with busts of Stalin, was like a play-room in an English school and, as far as I could make out, there was no difference in the programme. The directors trotted out the usual remarks about 'building Soviet character', games specially devised for 'a Communist State', 'a new understanding of an historic situation', but I suspect the activities were the same as prevailed in Winston Churchill's nursery eighty years ago. That does not mean to say they were bad and reactionary!

The dormitories were congested with beds and would not have been acceptable to Her Majesty's Inspectors, but I had to remind myself that the comparison should not be Russia and England, but Russia as it was when the Soviets came to power and Russia today. Even so, there was more space in this bedroom than in the ordinary Russian home. On the walls were photographs of Lenin and Stalin. What poor substitutes for the Good Shepherd with which the walls of my childhood are associated!

I told my guide I wanted to make a thorough inspection of

a Soviet school. A day was fixed and then, as so often happened, there was an inexplicable delay. I spent two hours in the Intourist office at the National Hotel kicking my heels, only to be told that it was not convenient and I must wait until the next day. I could never make out whether the delays were due to the creakings of a top-heavy bureaucratic machine, or to the determination of my guides to make sure that I only visited the show-pieces. So far as the school was concerned I specially asked that I should not be taken to a modern building, but to something more typical. When we eventually set off in the taxi we went to an ugly grey barracks in an outlying district. My companion suggested he would have preferred to have shown me a school more in keeping with the present educational programme, but he had bowed to my wishes and had chosen one which had no particular structural merits. In fact he successfully conveyed the impression of its anonymity by walking up and down the street twice before we found the entrance. He said he knew nothing about it except its numerical designation, No. 315. Whether he was indulging in a little camouflage or not, I don't know, but when in the plane which took me back to England I was reading Gordey's *Visa to Moscow*, I was interested to discover that he too was taken to school No. 315.

The headmaster, who had been teaching since Tsarist days, looked like a sergeant-major with a red face and an imposing moustache which curled at the ends. He gave me a charming welcome, took me to his study and proudly pointed to the Order of Lenin, the equivalent of a Knight of the Garter, on his lapel. He plied me with cigarettes which was unusual for a Communist. In fact he was the only member of the party who smoked in my presence during the whole of my stay. I told him I had been a schoolmaster and was wanting to learn as much as I could about Soviet education and I suggested we should conduct the conversation by the method of question and answer, and afterwards we could visit the classrooms.

'Very good, my friend. Whatever suits you. I am always pleased to welcome an Englishman to my school, especially one who has been a member of our profession. But before you begin, let me emphasize one thing—the aim of the Soviet school is to educate children for Soviet life in the Soviet State.'

'And how do you do that apart from your general teaching?' I asked.

'The Communist Party takes an active interest in school affairs. In a few minutes you will see boys in red ties and white shirts. They belong to the Pioneers which is the first step in mastering the Marxist understanding of society. The director of the Pioneers organizes their games and leisure activities and takes them on excursions to places of historic political interest in Moscow. When the boy is fifteen he leaves the Pioneers and joins, if he wishes, the Young Communist League. There are six million members in the Soviet Union, so not all those who want to join are admitted.'

'What does the Young Communist League teach him?'

'We'll take the official handbook for the answer. Here it is: "Members must strive with determination and with zest for the actualization of the policy of the Communist Party. Members must devote their energies to strengthening the Soviet régime, and to fighting against class enemies. A member's education and all his interests must prepare him for entering the party ranks." I cannot put it more clearly. Education does not stand by itself; it must be harnessed to the historic mission of our socialist society.'

Just how closely it was harnessed I was soon to discover. The pursuit of knowledge as an end in itself is a *bourgeois* myth. Knowledge is only knowledge if it finds a niche in a gigantic propaganda machine. If it does not fit, it must be made to fit, no matter what distortions and gymnastics may be necessary.

As I was anxious to avoid a Marxist lecture—already I had

had several—I steered the conversation to more general topics by asking the headmaster to give me the facts about his school.

'It was built in 1926. We have a thousand pupils, and fifty-two teachers, twenty of whom are men. We used to take boys and girls, but we no longer consider co-education desirable, so we have only boys.'

'But I thought your Government objected to the segregation of the sexes. We often do it in England, but then you regard us as hopelessly out of date with our wicked ideas on the inferiority of women.'

'Ah, my friend, you make a mistake. In our country segregation is based on a scientific fact. In a Soviet State a Soviet woman needs a special training which would be of little use to a Soviet man.'

I nodded wisely as though I was impressed with his propaganda twaddle and started on another line.

'Headmaster, when do the boys start their schooling? When do they leave? And how many sorts of schools are there in your country?'

'They come at seven, and leave at seventeen.'

'In that case they start two years later than we do in England, but they stay two years longer. Do they all remain until seventeen?'

'Yes, everybody.'

'Well, how does the country find sufficient people for unskilled jobs? If all children reach matriculation standard, as you say they do, they will want to go to the university or the technical college.'

'But you are mistaken. Not everybody reaches matriculation standard; only those who get into the top class and stay at school until seventeen.'

'But I thought you said everybody stayed.'

There was an awkward silence and my guide tried to gloss over the difficulty.

'A few leave school a little earlier, perhaps at fifteen or sixteen, but the majority stay.'

I still don't know the answer, but I suspect that, until accommodation is less restricted, only the brighter children do the full course, the others leaving at fourteen. In any case the curriculum is divided into ten grades. The first seven are compulsory, and twenty-five classes out of twenty-eight deal with them. For the top three grades, which are voluntary, there are only three classes. So it would seem that three to four classes are required for the annual intake, but as the age advances and numbers drop off one class is sufficient. If this calculation is right only a third of the children stay at school after the seventh grade is reached, which is usually at the age of fourteen.

The headmaster was reluctant to admit to over-crowding and I discovered the facts indirectly. He told me that junior boys had classes for twenty-four hours a week and seniors for thirty. 'That seems rather little,' I said, 'Four hours a day for the younger children and five hours for the older. When do you begin?'

'At half-past eight.'

'Well, it's five o'clock now. If the children only have these short hours, the school should have been closed at dinner time. Why are you still open?'

A pause. The guide came to the rescue.

'The point is, we are building many schools, but until the programme is fulfilled we have to be content sometimes with two shifts.'

'You mean that half come in the morning and half in the afternoon?'

'Well, yes.'

The headmaster looked uncomfortable and insisted that the hours were long enough.

'We think you are wrong in the West to work the children so hard.'

I decided not to pursue the argument.

Next we turned to salaries. Junior teachers get £240 p.a. and senior teachers £270. I said I thought the pay was poor in comparison with our Burnham scale. The headmaster replied that wage scales were fixed on an eighteen-hour week basis. Most teachers did overtime so they benefited appreciably from extra allowances.

I was impressed by the way parents are encouraged to take an interest in their children's education.

'In the old days parents didn't come to the school much,' the headmaster said, 'but after the Revolution the Government invited them to co-operate in the training of future Soviet citizens. May 1st is Parents' Day throughout the U.S.S.R. when mothers and fathers are expected to attend the celebrations at their children's schools. We always have a packed meeting and we explain the purposes of education. And twice a term we have smaller rallies, when we show parents around the school and explain new developments. In addition each teacher is available once a month in his classroom for any parent to talk over a child's progress. And if a boy slacks, seems to find the work too difficult, or is badly behaved we ask the father to discuss the problem with us so that together we can look for a solution. By these methods parents learn they are welcome at the school and that our job, if it is to be done successfully, must be shared with them.'

The school year begins on 1st September and ends on 24th May. Examinations are held during the first three weeks in June. There are two short breaks: winter, 31st December to 11th January; spring, 25th March to 1st April. During the long summer vacation the school is responsible for labour camps, expeditions, and visits to the seaside. I saw photographs and films of rest centres, log cabins in the mountains, sanatoria on the coasts of the Black Sea and always hundreds of cheerful, healthy children thoroughly enjoying themselves, looked after by the staff and the school doctor. A child is not compelled to spend his vacation with his schoolmates. He is free to stay at home or to join his parents for a private holiday, but about half of them avail themselves of the opportunities. In necessitous cases there is no charge, but usually parents make a contribution toward the cost in accordance with their income.

When the children remain in Moscow they can amuse themselves at the Central House of the Pioneers. The headmaster was enthusiastic and urged me to make a visit. It is indeed a remarkable institution and I marvelled at the cleverness with which the authorities sugar the Marxist pill. There seemed to be provision for every hobby. In one room professionals were teaching chess, and their many pupils were rapt in concentration. Near by were classes in water-colours and oils and another for sculpture. In each case the subjects were politically correct. The main hall was devoted to Marxist education. Portraits and busts of Lenin and Stalin, pictures of Russian generals, slogans, quotations and speeches and, of course, a large dose of 'peace' propaganda. Particularly impressive were the classes for ballet and dramatic art. The children reached a high standard and discussed their mistakes with leading actors and ballerinas. The machine shop was an answer to a schoolboy's prayer. Engineers taught the children how to construct machines, aeroplanes, motor-cars and boats and a girl had built a cruiser sufficiently well to win a national prize. Another class was being initiated into the intricacies of colour photography and film-making. Perhaps the most remarkable feature was the short-wave broadcasting station which had been built by the youngsters and was continuously manned by them.

No wonder the headmaster of No. 315 school was proud of the Central House of the Pioneers. He had every reason to be. In his own school he is keen to link theory with practice. As he took me around the building I was struck by the practical equipment. It was lavish. Each department had its film library and projector. There were gadgets for astronomy, geography and agriculture. There were generous collections of maps, globes, engineering tools, minerals, charts, and diagrams. In the natural-science laboratory the boys grew their own plants and kept birds, mice, guinea-pigs and rabbits. The carpentry department was specially well equipped and the work showed signs of real artistry.

I am somewhat critical of modern educational theories and I think the so-called Activity Methods have done a deal of harm in our own schools, but in Russia they have learnt how to combine theory with practice and free-expression with discipline. I asked the headmaster about general standards of discipline. Apparently in the early days of the Revolution the children had had the upper hand and Comrade Teacher had to be careful in his dealings with them. He was the servant, not the master. But experience has wrought a change. In any case the hail-fellow-well-met attitude has disappeared, and the boys treated the staff with proper respect.

'What happens if a boy misbehaves?' I asked.

'He is reprimanded by his teacher.'

'And if that doesn't work?'

'He is sent to me.'

'And what do you do?'

'I point out the seriousness of the offence, and I tell him that if he persists he will not be a worthy citizen.'

'If you think it justifiable, do you cane him?'

'No, corporal punishment is forbidden. It is an evil relic of the capitalist State. No child is thrashed in Russia today.' (I did not tell him that I had seen a mother in a Moscow park grab a boy who had torn his trousers on a tree, put him over her knee and spank him soundly!)

'But suppose he won't listen to you, what then?'

'I send for the parents and ask for their co-operation. In really bad cases the boy will be suspended or sent away.'

Judging by the deference shown by the youngsters to the

headmaster, I don't think they would relish a visit to his study, even for a pi-jaw.

I shall always remember the school corridor along which I was taken. It was lined with aspidistras and above each plant was a portrait of Stalin. I felt as though I were in a continental cathedral looking at the stations of the Cross. Each day, as the boys move to and from their classrooms, they see the great Leader in every conceivable posture. How bored they must get with that face! It was even worse in the Assembly Hall which reminded me of a Communist Party headquarters on May Day. Vast portraits of Lenin and Stalin on the walls; busts of Lenin and Stalin on marble pedestals; quotations from Lenin and Stalin in frames; sickles and hammers galore. Red curtain on the stage; red covers on the table; red plush on the seats. 'Here we assemble for the great Soviet celebrations,' the headmaster told me. I was not surprised.

On our way to the library I noticed the wall newspapers. Each class has its own paper called 'Our Word', giving information about the achievements of its members and making mention of several topics of current interest. And, of course, there were the usual Stalin quotations. Some of the papers were illustrated and the cartoons were amusing. The main wall was reserved for the school paper which was really well done. It gave details of old boys, a commentary on school events, and information about schools elsewhere.

The library had, so I was told, thirty thousand volumes, but I suspect that many were text-books for daily use. I noticed rows and rows of Marxist authors and even more shelves set apart for the speeches and writings of Stalin. Most of the names conveyed nothing to me, but Shakespeare, Dickens, Shelley, Zola and Victor Hugo had their places. The librarian assured me that the boys were 'greedy for books' and in their thirst for knowledge made considerable use of the lending department. In addition to the school library, each class has its own library of two thousand books.

As time was getting short I asked the headmaster if I might visit a classroom. He readily agreed and we called on the geography master. The boys, about thirty in number, stood up as I entered and when the headmaster told them who I was they said, smiling pleasantly: 'Good afternoon, sir.' I asked them to be seated, and requested the master to ignore my presence and go ahead with his lesson. In an English school the children would certainly have turned round at intervals to look at the foreigner, but not the Russian boys. They have beautiful manners.

My guide acted as interpreter. The lesson dealt with fruit growing in Georgia. The master described the trees, their cultivation and their products. He described conditions on the collective fruit farms and the lives of the workers. When he had finished his talk, two boys lowered a screen, and three more operated the projector. It was a simple, well-produced film illustrating the talk.

When I got up to leave, the senior boy made a charming speech and asked me to convey their greetings to the children of England, expressing the hope that they would work for peace. I assured them that everybody in England hated war and the British Government was doing its best to work for peace. The boys asked the master if they might have my autograph, and I readily signed their books.

The headmaster was reluctant to let me go as he said I had not seen half the school. I told him I was already two hours late for my next engagement. But he would not take 'no' for an answer. 'Come back to my study for one more cigarette and meet some of the staff.' I did not feel I could refuse, so I went to his room and talked with his senior assistants.

And then I had an idea. I had asked to attend an English lesson but was told that there wasn't one that afternoon. I let the matter rest until the moment of my departure.

'May I see the textbook from which you teach English?'
It was produced. It is on my study desk now, and I shall

have occasion to refer to it later when I attempt to describe the appalling propaganda in Russian schools directed against Great Britain. Our local Communists dismiss most of our charges against the Soviet machine as lies of the capitalist Press, but they cannot explain away this book which is a wicked tissue of misrepresentation and lies and proves, beyond the least possible doubt, that the minds of young Russians are systematically poisoned.

But I don't want to leave school No. 315 on an unpleasant note. There was much to dislike but much to admire. The headmaster was a skilled Marxist propagandist, but, according to his lights, he was interested in education and he cared for his boys. He was proud of his achievements and he was keen for me to appreciate them. I told him I should be glad to welcome him in England and show him some of our schools. He said he would like to come. I believe he would, but he won't be allowed. He said he was a schoolmaster before the Revolution. I wonder if he ever wonders why it was that in the evil days of the Tsar he could have visited this country at will and why it is that since the 'liberation' he is no longer free to be a guest in my house.

Whether or not as many boys and girls go to the university as the headmaster would have me believe, Moscow University is an astonishing place. It is set on the Lenin Hills outside Moscow and has a wonderful view of the city. It is so large that it is really a township in itself. But—and this is what I want to stress—four years ago not a stone had been laid. This incredible building which, had it been in England, would have been in construction for at least a quarter of a century, has been completed in less than a thousand days. But to describe it as a building is misleading, because it is a collection of buildings, thirty-seven in all.

The main block, made of great concrete slabs, has thirty-two floors. At the centre is the impressive assembly hall, with its marble colonnades, acoustic plates covered with silk and magnificent furniture. At the far end is a platform which is used each Saturday for a symphony orchestra. Above it is a vast mosaic of the Red flag in two and a half million pieces of stone. On either side, in letters of gold, are quotations from the speeches of Stalin to the effect that learning must lead to public action—'an intellectual must be an activist for the benefit of his country'.

My guide took me to the lecture rooms which were superb. There are two hundred. Special arrangements are made for deaf students. Every contraption likely to help a lecturer is laid on.

We took the lift, one of many, to the living quarters. I don't think I have ever travelled so rapidly and I felt ill on arrival. Each set has two bed-sitting rooms, a shower, a lavatory, a pantry. The dons have more spacious flats with every comfort. At the end of each corridor is a kitchen so that students who prefer to eat in their rooms can cook for themselves. I asked to be taken to some rooms in occupation so that I could talk with the undergraduates, but, as usual, I was told it was not convenient. The authorities are determined that the citizens of tomorrow shall not be contaminated by the evil influences of Western democracy.

Back to the lift and an even more frightening journey to the ground floor where we inspected a canteen. It was a large bright room and could seat a thousand. Some students brought their sandwiches with them, but most ordered the menu which was adequate and cheap.

My guide introduced me to an official who was accustomed to answer the questions of English visitors. I made the most of the opportunity.

'How many students are here?'

'Eight thousand now, but when we celebrate the two hundredth anniversary of Moscow University we shall have twelve thousand.'

'Is that the final figure?'

'Certainly not. You see the university is scattered through-out the city. Bit by bit each department will be transferred here and, when the whole job is done, we shall accommodate forty thousand. And, of course, there are the dons and research students as well. Three thousand are in residence at the moment. You must be sure to have a look at the crèches and kindergartens for the children of the professors, and I think you will be interested in the telephone exchange, electric power station and theatre. When you looked at the building outside I don't suppose you thought we are like a city of our own.'

'No, I did not. It is a remarkable achievement. But it must have cost a lot of money. How much do you reckon it costs to keep a student here for a year?'

'£500.'

'Is it free?'

'Yes. But each student makes a symbolic offering of £10 per annum. It's very little, but it will probably mean he will have to work for a fortnight in his summer holiday to get it, either on a farm or in a factory. We find people value things more if they contribute something.'

'I would be grateful if you would tell me something about the rates of pay for the teaching staff. What would a junior don get?'

'£750.'

'And a senior, a head of a department?'

'£3,000.'

'And what about the people at the very top, like our vice-chancellors at a British university?'

'£4,500.'

'Have you a large English faculty?'

'Yes. Students are encouraged to learn your language.'

'May I listen to a lecture?'

'I am sorry, but there isn't one this afternoon.'

'Well, may I see some of the books used for teaching?'

63

'Yes, come to the bookstall.'

I turned over the pages, and for the first time since I arrived in Russia I felt really angry. 'The whole thing is one damned lie. You people have the effrontery to say you want peace with us and you cram the heads of your young people with lampoons, caricatures and misrepresentations of my country. How can we have decent relationships when you are always injecting your future citizens with this sort of poison.'

'I am afraid I don't know what you mean.'

'What I mean is this. This book is supposed to give your students a factual account of England today. I cannot find one sentence in the book that even approximates to the truth. All countries are guilty of propaganda, but there's a difference between propaganda and sheer downright lying. Next time an Englishman visits your university you would be wise to withdraw this book. Even the "fellow-travellers", who delight in abusing the country of their origin, won't swallow this.'

My guide, not surprisingly, was somewhat embarrassed and suggested I should visit the theatre. Tempers subsided and we found ourselves in a non-controversial atmosphere looking, with admiration, at the latest technical devices. It was a very good theatre, but I couldn't help wondering about the nature of the plays performed in it. My friend, reading my thoughts, remarked: 'We often perform Dickens.'

'*Oliver Twist*, I suppose.'

Next to the libraries which would be a credit to any university. The rooms were bright and comfortable and the arrangements for obtaining books sensible. A student places his request on a miniature escalator and a few minutes later the book arrives. There was no hanging around shelves or queuing at an office. I noticed the technical magazines and felt a ray of hope. In spite of all the propaganda the students are able to communicate with the minds of the West and pick up incidental knowledge. If they have any perception they

A station on the Moscow Underground

An Orthodox priest conducting a service in Moscow

Alexis, Patriarch of All Russia, casting his vote during a civic election

must wonder how a country, which is supposed to be reduced to misery and squalor, can produce first-class brains and first-class machines. Their appreciation of our culture is dim, but they are bound to become aware of its existence. And the awareness should ultimately lead to questioning. As I left the university for my hotel, I turned over in my mind the possible outcome of Soviet education. Although much of it is scientific and technical, yet minds are being tempered and discrimination and analysis will inevitably follow. Tyranny has always tried to dominate the educational machine, but a point is usually reached beyond which domination is no longer a possibility. It may well be that Moscow University is already sowing the seeds of a more liberal future, a future which will see the human spirit cast aside its shackles. At the moment every scrap of learning from the kindergarten to the lecture hall is made to fit into the Marxist jig-saw, but the day may come when the mind will pass judgement on the jig-saw.

Chapter Four

THE CHURCH

'REVEREND Mervyn Stockwood with love in Christ. Alexis, Patriarch of Moscow and all Russia.' This inscription, written in the Patriarch's hand, appears on the frontispiece of the Bible given to me by His Holiness on a memorable occasion to which I shall refer later. It is a singularly beautiful copy of the Scriptures, with chain references, outline studies and charts—printed in the United States of America. It holds a place of special honour in my study, standing next to the little pocket Testament which was found on the bedside table of Archbishop William Temple on the day he died. I have been interested in the Orthodox Church for many years, long before I concerned myself with political matters. As a boy I read its history and at the university I made up my mind that one day I should see the Patriarch. This Bible bears witness to the fulfilment of a young man's ambition—one of the very few; more important, it is a constant reminder of a distinguished Head of a great Church.

There is a deal of confusion in people's minds about the Church in Russia. Some imagine it is non-existent, others that it is brutally persecuted, while our 'fellow-travellers' assure us that it is free and flourishing. All are wrong.

The Soviet Government has two policies, long-term and short. The former has as its goal the elimination of all forms of religion; the latter seeks to achieve a temporary *modus vivendi* with believers on the assumption that so long as there is a Church it is better to have it as an ally than an enemy. Let's have a look at them.

A few weeks before I arrived in Moscow a significant article appeared in the Soviet Press on the Marxist way to overcome religion. It was written by P. Kolonitskii. It's worth giving some substantial extracts because it neatly sums up the ideological attitude toward religious faith—an attitude which has never changed and never will change so long as Marxism remains Marxism.

'Religion represents one of the most persistent relics of slavery and exploitation. It is one of the most notable expressions of the downtrodden and unenlightened state of the masses common to any society built on the deprivation of rights and the exploitation of the workers. In our country the causes which generate religion do not exist. With the removal of social oppression we eliminated long ago the strongest and deepest roots of religion.'

'Millions of Soviet people who were formerly believers have cast aside religious views and habits, while the young generation which has grown up under the Soviet system is, as a rule, completely free from religious prejudices. However, some individuals have not yet abandoned their religious convictions, which will not disappear of their own accord, but as a result of the active political educational work of the Communist Party.'

'It is frequently asked whether, under our conditions, the assertion that religion is harmful is not out of date. The Church in our country as a rule adopts a perfectly loyal attitude toward the Soviet system, and the most outstanding representatives of the Orthodox Church are among the active fighters for peace. Is it not time, therefore, to change our attitude toward religion, and to cease to regard it as a reactionary ideology?'

'Religion, by the force of its slavish, exploiting nature, remains, and always will remain, a reactionary ideology, incompatible with the ideology of a fighter for Communism. All its dogmas and basic principles boil down to one thing—

that transitory, earthly life is troublesome and trivial compared with the eternal heavenly paradise. Thus servants of the Church, preaching belief in God, do an evil work, since they sow ignorant ideas in the minds of believers and thereby, willingly or unwillingly, oppose the cause of Communist education and the struggle for Communism as a whole.'

'The harmful effect of religion on the work of education in Communist morals is obvious. If Communist morals urge the Soviet people forward, mobilize and multiply their forces in the struggle for Communism, religion pulls them back and seizes hold of all that is old and has outlived its time.'

'Marxists understand that it is impossible to do away with religion by means of administrative constructions. Under our Socialist conditions religion will not disappear of itself. It clings to life and hampers our forward movement. Religion always has a firmer hold in places where there is not enough persistent and systematic work in the dissemination of political and scientific knowledge. The vitality of religious prejudices on various parts of our country is due frequently to the neglect of cultural educational work and to the lack of systematic natural scientific atheistic propaganda. The task in the sphere of atheistic propaganda consists in driving religion out of the minds of believers by the light of scientific and political knowledge.'

'Religion has always been the expression and practice of passivity. As a relic of the past, it is not compatible under our conditions with the active struggle of the workers for the victory of the new life. For the Soviet people there is no necessity to console themselves with hopes of an imaginary bliss. By their daily work they are creating and multiplying happiness on earth. The time is not far distant when no trace will remain of the relics of the past, including religion.'

So much for Mr Kolonitskii. I hope readers have marked, learnt and inwardly digested what he says because it is immensely important if we are to understand the religious situation in the Soviet Union. Muddle-headed idealists, who are shown by their guides well-filled churches in Moscow, return to Britain under the impression that the Communists have changed their mind about religion. Nothing could be farther from the truth. Political expediency may demand temporary changes in practical policies, but Marxism is, and always must be, the inveterate enemy of Christianity because of its denial of the existence of God and of the reality of Spirit.

Now let's see how the suggestions of Mr Kolonitskii are applied. Mr N. G. Dairi, a master in a secondary school on the outskirts of Moscow, contributes a revealing article on anti-religious propaganda in the official educational journal, *Teaching of History in Schools*, No. 4. Children must be taught three things about religion:

1. That religion is dependent on material conditions and does not correspond to any deep and lasting psychological human need.

2. That religion and the Church, particularly the Roman Church, have always played a reactionary part in social life and that there is a fundamental antagonism between religious and Communist morality.

3. That religion and science are irreconcilable.

Mr Dairi then suggests how these points should be made. A teacher must not give any objective picture of the real nature and content of Christianity lest it be dangerous to his purpose. 'Facts about religious cults, dogmas, festivals, rites, must be selected very skilfully, otherwise one may start putting out propaganda for religion.'

The place of religion in different types of society must be explained in such a way as to explode the possibility of a supernatural origin. For example, in primitive society, according to Mr Dairi, men had no religion. It was not invented until men felt the need to explain their powerlessness in the face of nature. Similarly in discussing the early Slavs, it was the Slavs themselves who created the agricultural and tribal deities to resolve the perplexities of their communal life.

So far as the conversion of Russia to Christianity is concerned, the teacher must make it clear that it was the appendage of the feudal system. The rulers wanted to find something to justify their exploitation of the poor, and the people had to be given a faith that would help them to tolerate their appalling conditions by teaching them submission here and happiness hereafter. A careful selection of the sayings of Jesus will prove the point, especially if it is supplemented by a potpourri of Church history.

Mr Dairi concludes with an illustration in the art of teaching atheism. The subject is the Stenka Razin rising in the seventeenth century. The teacher must emphasize that the 'Church supported the ghastly vengeance against the insurgents in the region of Arzamas, where about eleven thousand peasants were executed. I attach great importance to showing the courage of Razin during interrogation. "Why did Razin behave like this?" I ask the children, on whom Razin's courageous behaviour makes a tremendous impression. "What gave him the very great courage which astonished everybody?" And I answer: "His great love for the people, whose son he was, and his unquenchable hatred of their oppressors. It is this hero, whose memory is cherished by the people, on whom the Church pronounced a curse! This curse was repeated every year in all churches during centuries of Tsarist domination."'

To what extent has this atheistic campaign been successful? It is difficult to say. I asked my guide what he knew about Jesus and the Scriptures and he replied: 'Nothing.'

'But surely you must have learnt something?' I remarked. 'After all, even if Jesus was nothing more than a teacher, he has made sufficient impact upon the world to demand serious attention. At least he should be grouped with Plato, Aristotle and Marcus Aurelius.'

'That's where we disagree with you. Plato, Aristotle and Aurelius were living people, but Jesus of Nazareth is a mythical personage, invented by the oppressing class.'

'And what about the Bible? Did the bosses write that?'

'Yes.'

'How much of it have you read?'

'Very little.'

'Do you remember anything?'

'Yes. A bit which tells the workers who have been hit across the face by their oppressors to turn the other cheek.'

On another occasion I met a theatrical critic in the rooms of the Mexican minister. I asked her if she knew what Christianity was about. She replied that she was completely ignorant except that she had been given to understand it was a collection of fairy tales which had long since been discredited. As for the Church, she had been taught at school that it was the Tsar's most effective weapon for perpetuating squalor, misery and illiteracy.

I often had discussions with the clerks at the National Hotel and the Intourist guides. Within a few days we became good friends and I consequently teased them about their atheism. Walking into their office I would describe myself as the local magician who was inventing a new superstition to enslave the workers. I used to tell them about the Church and my beliefs. They listened with kindly humour but said they didn't believe a word of it. They were entirely ignorant of all philosophy and ethical systems. Idealism in any shape or form was nonsense, and nothing mattered except the classless society of Marx. One day we talked about psychic phenomena, and I asked them what they thought about it. 'You can dismiss Christianity as bunk, but how do you account for the mystical experiences to which many can testify?'

'They can be explained psychologically.'

'Well, what about spiritualism?'

'What do you mean?'

'Haunted houses, spooks and table turning—and the like. I'm not saying that I believe in them as the spiritualists do, but even if most of them are frauds, there's usually something left which needs to be explained.'

'There aren't any haunted houses in Russia—at least there haven't been since the Revolution.'

'Now I know why the ghost goes West!'

Yes, it's as simple as that. The Communist Government says there is no God, so there isn't. Marx explains everything, and dialectical materialism has eliminated the need for idealistic philosophy and theology. But the extraordinary fact is, people of all ages go to Church. In spite of the atheistic propaganda which faces the Soviet citizen at every turn, religion persists. In most cases it is due to the tradition of the family, but not always. I was told of factory workers, scientists and doctors who had become Christians by asking questions and receiving instruction from their friends. Religious propaganda, unlike atheistic propaganda, is not permitted and the clergy must be careful what they say outside their church buildings, but there is nothing to prevent a man from going to church and learning what he can from the worship and the sermon.

The result of the short-term policy may seem, at a first glance, to deny what I have said, as the Communist authorities appear to connive at religion. In fact there is no contradiction. The Government is convinced that religion is disappearing and eventually will be eliminated. Meanwhile there is no point in antagonizing the Christian minority, especially as, during the transition, the Church can be made to serve a political end. Moreover, experience has shown the foolhardiness of making martyrs. After the Revolution the Government sponsored anti-God demonstrations, murdered priests, transported Christians to Siberia and ridiculed and blasphemed the Church. The result was different from what the Communists had expected. Some defaulted under duress, but the majority remained loyal. And, what is more important, the people as a whole began to admire the Church as they never had before: they were not practising Christians themselves, but they detested the vulgar, and often barbaric, persecution of a law-abiding minority. So Stalin called off the attack, and the clergy were gradually given back their democratic rights. Ration cards and the franchise returned to the vicarage and the anti-God museums were closed. Then came the purges. Nobody knows the cause. A book was recently published giving seventeen possible explanations, but it is anybody's guess. For some obscure reason Stalin, perhaps in a fit of megalomania—and I believe that he was basically crazy—decided to liquidate the leaders of the régime, the intelligentsia, the people in responsible positions. Inevitably the Church suffered along with many others and was condemned as an enemy of the people. Then came the war. Stalin had the sense to realize that a national emergency demands a united nation, otherwise the disaffected become likely candidates for a Fifth Column. Once again the anti-Church campaign was called off. What is more, the Government was compelled to realize that many soldiers were not prepared to go into battle without the consolation of the sacraments and the blessing of the Church. Whatever our private views may be about the rightness of the Church to identify itself with a war effort, the fact is the Orthodox Church, no less than the Church of England, supplied the spiritual cement. In both cases the Governments were pleased.

And there were other considerations. Stalin knew that the Allies had described the war against Hitler as a holy crusade. Now there was an embarrassing situation. The allies were yoked with a Government which had recently made a pact with Hitler and was avowedly atheistic. In order to appease the Allies, Stalin had to appease their religious prejudices. In short the Soviet Government, without in any way changing its basic attitude, knew that for temporary reasons of expediency it had to obtain the support of a Church it had recently persecuted.

That was not all. Stalin was shrewd enough to consider the future. He had already planned that the Balkan countries should eventually come under the domination of Moscow, and as he did not wish the Churches in these countries to look to the Patriarch of Constantinople, the leading bishop of the Orthodox Church, for leadership, he decided to increase the prestige of the Patriarch of Russia in order to make Moscow, not Constantinople, the centre of the Orthodox world. In the circumstances it is not surprising that the Patriarch of All The Russias left the little log cabin he had occupied on the outskirts of Moscow and took over the German Embassy. Naïve Westerners thought Stalin had changed his views; the more realistic knew he was playing political chess.

The Archbishop of Canterbury gave me a letter of introduction to the Patriarch. I told my guide and asked him to arrange a meeting with His Holiness, but was informed that he was out of Moscow. That was the usual reply. Whenever I wanted to see anybody who could give me useful information he was invariably out of Moscow and, as no telephone directory was published and personal contacts were prohibited, I could do nothing about it. But in this instance I was determined to get my own way. This is how I did it. One Saturday evening I asked my guide to take me to Moscow Cathedral for the customary service. As the building was full I was taken to the sanctuary where I saw the dean. 'Good evening, Mr Dean,' I said. 'I have a letter from the Archbishop of Canterbury for His Holiness the Patriarch. Is His Holiness in Moscow?'

'Yes he is,' said the dean. 'And as tomorrow is the feast

of St Alexis he will preside at High Mass, supported by many of his bishops.'

That was good enough for me. On Sunday morning I celebrated Holy Communion at the American Embassy and then hastened to the cathedral before returning to the Embassy for morning service. It was an astonishing sight. The place was packed: it reminded me of Piccadilly in the rush hour or Twickenham station before the Varsity match. As there are no pews in an Orthodox church, the people stood. They were so closely jammed together and it was impossible to raise an elbow, still less to move and, as the service lasts three hours, there can be no escape. The cathedral authorities estimated the congregation at twelve thousand. I was taken to a side door and given a place by the screen where I had an admirable view. I scrutinized the congregation as I was anxious to study its composition. My guides had told me that only old people, survivors of the Tsarist days, went to church and the young had nothing to do with religion. This did not apply to this particular congregation: all ages were represented and the proportion of men was greater than in England. I noticed dozens of uniforms and near me was a batch of servicemen, officers and other ranks. At least half the congregation must have been born since the Revolution and have grown up in an atheistic environment.

The service began with the ceremonial dressing of the Patriarch. An arena was cordoned off in the centre of the building and His Holiness, dressed in flowing black, was led to his throne. It reminded me of the coronation service in Westminster Abbey. The bishops approached the throne in threes, bearing his superb archiepiscopal vestments of cloth of gold. When he was fully attired his chaplains mounted the steps with a comb, whereupon the Patriarch stood and titivated his hair and beard. It was a magnificent sight. He then left his throne and passed through the screen to his place at the altar. As he approached me I, dressed in cassock, surplice and stole, made a profound bow which he acknowledged. A few minutes later the dean appeared and assured me of the Patriarch's greetings. I handed to him the Archbishop of Canterbury's letter, with the request that he should pass it on to His Holiness.

As the dignitaries were temporarily out of view, eyes began to stray in my direction and it was not long before attention was focused on me. My dress made it evident I was a Western priest and I was greeted with hundreds of smiles. It was suggested to me that I should bless them so I raised my hand and made the sign of the cross over those who stood near me. Others noticed what was happening and hundreds more looked at me, signed themselves and bowed in preparation for the benediction. It was a moving moment and one realized how powerless is an iron curtain in the family of Jesus Christ.

Next day I innocently informed the Intourist chief that the Patriarch had returned to Moscow and I hoped I should be able to see him.

'I will tell you tomorrow,' replied nice Mr Rogov—how he loved that phrase!

'But, Mr Rogov, I must see the Patriarch and I am depending upon you to fix it.'

'Perhaps I shall know this afternoon.'

The answer came after lunch. 'I am sorry, the Patriarch is too busy to see you.' I did not believe it and I decided to play for high stakes.

'Mr Rogov, this is serious. The Archbishop of Canterbury has requested His Holiness to give me an audience as there are matters between our respective Churches to be discussed. If it were only myself, I would accept your decision, but I cannot allow the Primate of all England to be insulted. What is more, when I return to Britain I should have to give publicity to the facts and they will hardly reflect credit upon your peace campaign.'

Mr Rogov looked serious. 'We shall see. I will talk with you tomorrow.'

I am not sure who arranges these things—perhaps a brass hat in the Soviet foreign office, or a network of civil servants. But Mr Rogov went to work and on the following morning informed me that His Holiness had reconsidered the matter and had decided he could spare me five minutes on the following Thursday. My battle was almost won, but not quite. I badly wanted to take with me an interpreter from the British Embassy to ensure a correct translation and to make an independent record of the conversation. I knew that, if I were dependent upon a Communist official, things might be misconstrued and I might be held responsible for statements I had never made. I decided to make a frontal attack.

'I am most grateful to you, Mr Rogov, for taking so much trouble. But please do not bother about guides or transport because, as I shall call on the Patriarch in my official capacity, the British Ambassador will supply me with an embassy car and an accredited interpreter. I realize, of course, your authorities may require government representatives to be present at the interview, but that is no business of mine.'

Poor Mr Rogov. He could hardly refuse, especially as I had called his bluff about the Soviet snoopers.

James Bennett, of the British Embassy, and I arrived at the Patriarchate, the former German Embassy, at 12.45 p.m. We were met by the administrative director, Father Kolchitsky, with whom we talked for a quarter of an hour. After exchanging the usual courtesies we sat around the table in the visitors' room. Father Kolchitsky asked for an agenda. In fact I had no agenda as my visit was private and informal, except that the Archbishop of Canterbury had directed me to convey his personal greetings and had expressed the hope that my visit would be mutually beneficial. But as I had to give a quick answer, I wrote down three things which I knew to be of particular interest to Churchmen in Britain—the possibility of the Russian Orthodox Church sending representatives to the World Council of Churches; the strengthening of relationships between the Anglican and Orthodox Churches; general information.

The World Council of Churches is a comparatively new organization to which most Christian bodies, excluding the Roman Church, send representatives. The Orthodox Churches in non-Communist countries play their part, but not the Russian Church for the simple reason that the Soviet Government will not allow it. The Anglican Church is anxious to have the co-operation of the Orthodox Church, because, apart from itself, most of the bodies are Protestant insofar as they are non-traditional. The presence of the Russian Church would strengthen the traditional Catholic position and give the World Council more balance. But I quickly discovered I was on a sticky wicket. Father Kolchitsky, a clever diplomat, said the matter was under review but, as it was so complex, an early decision was unlikely. 'A further difficulty', he said, 'is our fear that the World Council of Churches is subjected to political influences, and the Orthodox Church keeps clear from political entanglements.'

'With respect, Father, I venture to differ. The World Council is an ecclesiastical body and deals with matters of mutual interest to all the Churches. If, by any chance, you should disagree with the views expressed by other people, you are fully entitled to make clear your own position.'

'I see your point, Canon Stockwood, but I can give no answer.'

'Would the Russian Church like to receive an invitation to the next Assembly?'

'It is, of course, always pleasant to receive invitations.'

We passed to the next item. I suggested to Father Kolchitsky that although the relationships between the two Churches were cordial, we did not see enough of one another. 'For instance it would be helpful if our clergy and laity exchanged visits.'

'Have you any suggestions?'

'What about beginning with our leaders? I have no authority to commit the Archbishop of Canterbury, but I am sure he would consider visiting Russia, especially if the Patriarch would come to us.'

'That is an agreeable suggestion which we can discuss more fully with His Holiness in a few minutes.'

'Is there likely to be difficulty with the Government? Would the necessary visas be granted?'

'In the Soviet Union, Canon Stockwood, the State and the Church are separate and do not interfere in one another's business.'

We came to the third item—general information.

'Father Kolchitsky, I want to ask you many things about the Russian Church as we know so little. May I begin with theological colleges? The future of any Church obviously depends upon its manpower. I understand that for some years you were not allowed to have theological colleges. What is the position today?'

'We have two academies and ten seminaries. The academies cater for the advanced courses, the seminaries for the ordinary parish priest. In each of them we have about two hundred and fifty students. The course lasts eight years and the ages range from eighteen to fifty.'

'Have you sufficient candidates? In Britain we have a serious shortage and we are having to close down parishes.'

'Quite the contrary. We have more men than jobs and we have not sufficient room in the colleges for those who would like to train.'

'That is most encouraging. And how do you manage about text-books? Obviously you need specialized technical books and I don't suppose the Government permits its printing presses to turn out theological works. Incidentally, how about the Bible?'

'The Patriarchate has its own publishing department and

we have sufficient text-books in circulation. As for the Bible, the Church is in possession of a large stock printed in 1914. The shops cannot sell them, but they may be borrowed from the churches or passed from hand to hand.'

'What happens when the reserves run out?'

'We can print more on our own press. There is nothing to stop us.'

The clock on the mantelpiece struck one and almost immediately a butler entered the room to say the Patriarch awaited us in his study.

Alexis, who is short and stocky, was sitting at his desk, clothed in a black soutane, with a white mitre on his head. As we entered he arose and greeted us with a charming smile and a handshake. Father Kolchitsky took a seat on his right, and James Bennett faced him. At the back of the room were two men in civilian clothes; they said nothing and I suspect they were government snoopers.

I wish I could describe Alexis adequately, because he is one of the world's most astonishing men. He was a bishop before the Revolution and an aristocrat. Most of his contemporaries in Church and State disappeared long ago, but he still keeps his head—perhaps because he knows, better than most, how to keep his head! I am sure he is an extraordinarily deft diplomat and I can imagine his detractors dismissing him as a crafty fox. Crafty he may be, and perhaps must be, but I am sure that, although he does not wear his spirituality on his sleeve, his one desire is to serve the Church. For years he has played a dangerous game and, being a brilliant bargainer, he has won concessions which a generation ago would have seemed impossible. What he has had to pay for them nobody knows with certainty; some think thirty pieces of silver. Alexis, I suspect, would, with his enchanting smile, admit to twenty-nine and, at the same time, with his incredibly knowing eye, make it clear that the only piece which really mattered was still in his hand. Whatever may be the truth about his character and his intentions, I liked the man and, rightly or wrongly, I felt that beneath the wily politician and experienced ecclesiastic was a simple follower of Christ who had not forgotten how to say his prayers.

The Patriarch began the conversation by asking after the Archbishop of Canterbury and speaking in warm terms of the Church of England. He told me how pleased he had been to see me at the cathedral on the previous Sunday, and how glad he was to welcome me at his house. After these pleasantries we returned to the agenda. Father Kolchitsky summarized my remarks about the World Council of Churches, but the Patriarch was careful not to commit himself beyond saying that the Orthodox Church was glad to receive invitations.

When I mentioned possible exchange of visits, Alexis said that the presence of Dr Fisher in Moscow would bring the greatest pleasure to the Russian Church.

'I am glad to know it, Your Holiness,' I said. 'But we should hope the visit, if it materialized, would be reciprocated. I am in no way authorized to commit the Archbishop, nor do I know whether he would feel able to accept an invitation, but it would doubtless help if you were willing to come to England.'

'How old is your Archbishop?'

'In his early sixties, I think.'

'But I am seventy-six, and it's more difficult for me to travel. And yet your Archbishop of York, who must be eighty or ninety, is very active. He seems to go all over the world. He is a great man.'

'I hope you will follow his example, and visit London.'

At this point Alexis saw I was making notes with my left hand. 'Do you always use your left hand?' he asked.

'Yes, Your Holiness, always—but especially when I am in left-wing countries.' He laughed loudly, and even the snoopers smiled.

I pressed the matter of exchanges. 'Leaving the leaders on

one side, what about an exchange of students at ecclesiastical seminaries?'

'I can see no difficulty. We should be pleased to welcome a few British students at the beginning of the next academic year. I am not sure about our students going to Britain as not many of them can speak the language.'

I decided not to make the obvious retort. After all even if the traffic has to be one way for the time being, it is, at least, a beginning.

'And now, Your Holiness,' I continued, 'I should like your permission to ask you questions on the general Church situation.'

'Carry on. Ask anything you like.'

'First, I should be grateful for some statistics. How many clergy and churches come under your jurisdiction?'

'There are twenty-five thousand churches in the Soviet Union and thirty-two thousand priests.'

'And how about bishops?'

'We have seventy-five.'

'What about stipends? This is a matter of real concern to us in England because a reason for the shortage of clergy is the comparatively low wage.'

'Our priests are well paid. In Moscow the scale is from £1,500 to £2,500. In the country it is less, but there is no hardship.'

'In that case, Your Holiness, I think I had better apply for a transfer because your men are paid four or five times as much as we are! But can you give me some tips as to how you get the money?'

'From the faithful. They give generously.'

In this connexion it must be remembered that the Government has closed many churches. In Moscow there used to be sixteen hundred churches; today there are fifty-five. That is why they are always crowded. The collections are inevitably considerable and the clergy benefit accordingly. If most of the churches in London were put out of commission and only a fraction left open, thousands would flock to them, and the clergy would be a deal wealthier than they are today.

The Russian priests certainly looked prosperous. Their clothes were made of good material and their footwear was above average. A few had expensive cars. It is said that Alexis is extremely wealthy, but he gives away a large part of his income to subsidize the country clergy.

As I had already been with the Patriarch for half an hour I thought the time had come to ask him about relationships with the State. I knew he would not talk about the early persecutions, the shootings, concentration camps, the withdrawal of ration cards and civic rights from the clergy, because that period had passed and, in the presence of the snoopers, it was best forgotten. So I confined myself to recent years.

'I understand, Your Holiness, that the relations between Church and State have taken a turn for the better. I don't want to press you for information if it would be embarrassing, but in England we are naturally interested, not least because it's difficult to get reliable information.'

'It's true we passed through a bad stage but that was some time ago. There has been—what shall I say?—a stabilization which has led to a reasonable understanding.'

'Am I right in supposing that when Stalin died you broadcast a tribute in your official capacity?'

'No. I have never broadcast, but perhaps you don't appreciate that there is no tradition of religious broadcasting in Russia. Nevertheless I did conduct a memorial service in the cathedral, because Stalin, besides being a great patriot, was much valued by the Church. I should like to repeat that —Stalin was much valued by the Church. He understood our position and whenever difficulties arose I found him most co-operative.'

When the interview was over I discussed with James Bennett this unexpected tribute. Both of us felt it was genuine, and not mere eyewash for the snoopers. Stalin is a back number since his successors took over and most people are careful to refrain from praising him. Perhaps the Patriarch and the dictator respected one another as bargainers; in any case Alexis appreciated Stalin's prodigious efforts to raise the living standards of the people and recognized him as a patriot.

My 'fellow-travelling' friends in Britain try to persuade me that a Christian can support a Marxist régime, so I decided to go to the horse's mouth.

'Your Holiness, what are your views on Marxism?'

The wily old man fixed me with his eye and said: 'Marxism—I really don't know anything about it.' And then, giving an infectious chuckle with a devastating wave of the hand, he exclaimed: 'It's all about politics, history and capital.'

'But do you feel it is compatible with Christianity?' I asked.

And here the Patriarch revealed himself in his true colours. He remained a statesman without compromising himself as a Christian. 'The Church is not concerned with politics, and, insofar as Marxism is a political matter, we pass no judgement. But when it comes to a materialistic analysis of man, there is, of course, a conflict between the two systems.'

'And what is the Church doing to combat materialism?' I inquired. 'Your children are brought up in atheistic schools and Christianity is ridiculed. I am distressed at the amount of ignorance I have found among some of your young people. They know nothing about God.'

'It is difficult. But the Orthodox Church has never been an evangelistic Church or a militant propagandist. We emphasize the importance of the liturgy, and we leave it to God to do the rest. But you must not think we are losing. We are always having inquiries. Professional men, engineers and scientists are abandoning their careers to enter our theological academies. A distinguished doctor, a Stalin prize-winner, joined the other day. I admit the dangers of materialism. People are so occupied with improving their living standards, they have little time for God. But that is not a weakness peculiar to the Soviet Union. Materialism seems to be as firmly entrenched in Britain and the United States.'

'That is true. The main difference between us is that we like to ignore the fact and pretend we are a Christian country.'

The interview had lasted an hour and a half and, much as I should have liked to have stayed, I felt the Patriarch had already been more than generous. I got up to go. Alexis beckoned to a butler who came forward with three packages. The first was a pectoral cross for the Archbishop of Canterbury; the second an exceptionally beautiful Bible for myself, and the third an assortment of books to which I shall refer in a later chapter.

Here is the letter which accompanied the cross. It is reproduced with Dr Fisher's permission.

The Patriarchate
Moscow

22 October 1953

Your Grace,

Beloved Brother in Christ,

I received with sincere love the Reverend Mervyn Stockwood, who transmitted me the greetings of Your Grace.

I was very glad to see him at our divine service in our Cathedral on Sunday the 18th October. I am sure that his impressions from all that he saw in our country and particularly in respect of our Church are favourable.

I send to Your Grace my cordially brotherly feelings and, as a token of our spiritual contact, clean as this rock crystal, I send to you a holy pectoral cross with an image of our Saviour. May He bless Your Grace, your Church and your people in peace and full prosperity.

Your loving brother in Christ,
Alexis.

Patriarch of Moscow and All Russia.

His Grace The Archbishop of Canterbury
Primate of All England
And Metropolitan.

After I had thanked the Patriarch for his gifts I knelt to receive his blessing and he led us to the hall to sign the visitors' book. A charming incident followed. The Patriarch suddenly withdrew and I imagined he had had more than enough of me and was hurrying off to work. But he came back with a small English testament in his hand for my young interpreter, James Bennett. James is at the beginning of his career and has only just joined the Embassy staff. I am sure he will treasure his Testament as a memento of an enthralling interview and a charming host.

Chapter Five

WORKERS' PARADISE

'THE task of the trade unions is to educate the workers in cultural and scientific development and to control the conditions of labour. Trade unions are the schools, of Communism and the handmaid of the Government.' That is how my conversation began with the bosses of Moscow's Transport House. I think it must be a quotation from a Marxist handbook because it was repeated in the same tone of voice as is used by a don at a Cambridge high table when saying a Latin grace.

There are thirty-nine unions in the Soviet Union. They cater for approximately forty million. Their function is not the same as the unions in the Western democracies.

My hosts greeted me in a vestibule which was well adorned with red flags and portraits of Stalin, before taking me to an exhibition hall for a display of safety gadgets. I know nothing about machinery so it would be useless for me to make comparisons. All I can say is that I was asked to put my hand into a fearsome-looking object which had two horribly sharp blades. I hesitated as I did not wish to return to England minus an arm. My guide set the example. When his finger was within two inches of the blades, the machine stopped dead. Having gained confidence, I followed suit. I was informed that dangerous machines must have a safety appliance which consists of two small lights which send out beams that automatically paralyse the works the moment an object intercepts them. No doubt there are similar gadgets

87

in this country, but as I rarely visit engineering firms I haven't seen one.

Parties of workers were being shown round the exhibition and I was impressed by the keenness of the guides. They were determined to generate enthusiasm for new processes and more efficient machinery. 'If we are to industrialize the Soviet Union successfully,' they said, 'the workers must understand our plans and toil intelligently to fulfil them. We are not like you in the West. We look upon the worker as a co-operator and we know we shall only get the best out of him if we take him into our confidence. This necessitates a two-way traffic. We explain everything to him, and we listen to his criticisms and welcome his suggestions. Many of the improvements you see here are the result of the inventions of the men at the bench.'

I was then plied with facts and figures and given sheaves of statistics. My brain was in a whirl, but I did get a general impression of the gigantic task which the Government had set itself in its efforts to modernize the country. As I have said before, a Westerner, in trying to assess the achievements of the Communist régime, must remember that the fair comparison is not the Russia and Britain of today, but Russia today and Russia in 1917. The fact is, in less than forty years a backward agricultural country has been industrialized and transformed, even though the standards are below ours. And scoffers should never forget that had Stalin been less successful the outcome of the recent war might have been different and Hitler would be in occupation of the Kremlin.

We went to the manager's room and sat at his table for an informal discussion.

'I want you to tell me about your unions. Do they differ from ours? Are they associated with the Government? How do they look after the workers?'

The manager answered by telling his secretary to pass me an English translation of the *Constitution of the Trade*

Unions in the U.S.S.R., and drawing my attention to particular paragraphs. I have the booklet in front of me as I write.

'First of all, Canon Stockwood, please look at these historic words of Comrade Stalin: "People in our country do not work for exploiters, for the enrichment of parasites, but for themselves, for their own class, for their own Soviet society." This means an entirely different attitude toward work. In a capitalist country the employers and the workers are enemies; in our country the employer is the worker and the worker the employer.'

'Why, then, do you have trade unions? If everybody is working happily together and there are no differences of interest between bosses and men, I should have thought your organizations were superfluous.'

'You are wrong. There are two main reasons. Turn to page four of the constitution. "In conformity with the interests of the working people and in order to strengthen the socialist system, citizens of the U.S.S.R. are guaranteed by law freedom of speech, freedom of the Press, freedom of assembly, and also the right to unite in public organizations. In the Soviet trade unions, which are a mass non-party public organization, workers and other employees of all occupations are united on a voluntary basis."'

'I don't see how that fits in with what you told me. All the same I'm interested to know you have the right to say what you like and to organize yourselves for your own purposes. I should like to know what would happen if you were to say a few abusive things about the Government and to organize an opposition to throw the Government out?'

'You are a *bourgeois* and you look at things from the point of view of the capitalist class. In a Communist country the Government and the workers are one. It would be impossible to have an opposition.'

'Why?'

'An opposition could only exist if we had enemies of the workers' State, wanting to restore capitalism. But there aren't any.'

'That's a delightfully honest confession and, in view of what you say, I don't think we can usefully pursue this particular line. Now let's have the second reason for your organizations.'

'The trade unions instil in their membership the spirit of Soviet patriotism and a Communist attitude to work; they engage in the Communist training of the working people and in advancing the culture and professional standards of the workers. They imbue their members with a sense of proletarian internationalism and fight for the unity of the international working-class movement and for lasting peace and democracy throughout the world. As Comrade Lenin said: "The trade unions are an educational organization, an organization for enlisting and training forces; they are a school of administration, a school of management, a school of Communism."'

'I hope you won't think me awkward and rude, but I haven't come here for a political lecture. I've made an exhaustive study of Marxism and I probably know as much about it as you. So please take that for granted, and let's get down to business. I want to know what the trade unions do. For instance, do they organize strikes?'

My hosts exploded—with laughter. 'Strikes? We never have strikes.'

'I thought not. In fact it never occurred to me that your freedom of speech and association went as far as that! All the same, why not? Sometimes a strike is a good thing, as it's the only weapon a worker has for getting justice.'

'But don't you see, Canon Stockwood, in a Communist State no worker wants to strike. The Soviet Union is a workers' State, and the workers, who give themselves justice, cannot strike against themselves. In the Communist vocabulary there is no such word as strike.'

'My friends, that's the richest remark I've heard since I've been in Russia. Let me repeat it: "In the Communist vocabulary there is no such word as strike." If your pals in Britain really believed that, they wouldn't know how to occupy their time because their lust for disrupting industry and organizing stoppages is insatiable.'

'In England it is different. Your workers have to strike. Their conditions are appalling.'

'In fact, they are a deal better off than yours and wouldn't tolerate your conditions of labour for an instant. But we won't argue about that. We'll steer clear of politics for a few minutes and confine ourselves to non-controversial topics. After that we will have another free for all.'

My hosts were enjoying themselves as much as I was. We were spoiling for a fight, but it was a good-natured tussle and, although we did not mince words, tempers remained calm and we laughed a lot. One of the reasons why I should like to go back to Russia is because I always felt that our divergent and usually contradictory views did not impair our personal relationships.

I directed the conversation into calmer waters. 'Tell me about sick benefits, holidays, and insurance schemes.'

'A worker pays one per cent of his monthly earnings, and providing his payments are not in arrears he enjoys many privileges. You will find them in the little book I gave you. Let's read what it says. "A member receives priority in the distribution of passes to rest homes, sanatoria and health resorts and also in placing his children in crèches and kindergartens; he receives free legal assistance; he and his family have the use of the trade union cultural and sports facilities." You have to remember these things when you try to assess Soviet wages. I expect in your country the workers have to pay for most of these things; in our country they are free.'

'I don't think you are right about my country because we have all sorts of insurance schemes and health services and, although you won't believe it, our workers are well protected. But I do admit you do more about holiday facilities than we do. Tell me, are these holidays free and do all workers take advantage of them?'

'They pay a little, perhaps a quarter of the cost; it depends on their circumstances. Not everybody likes this sort of a holiday, but most do and most have it.'

I'm afraid my informant was not truthful. I subsequently discovered from an official report published in *Pravda* that less than ten per cent of Soviet workers enjoyed these amenities. As the years go by more rest centres and sanatoria will be built, but it will be years before there are sufficient for the whole population. Even so, the Government can be justly proud for providing good holidays for two million of the population.

I asked about illness and retirement.

'In a Communist country the Government provides free medical treatment and when a worker falls ill his wages are paid in full.'

'We also have free medical treatment, but it is only some firms that make up wages when an employee is on the sick list.'

'That is bad. When a man is ill, he needs more money, not less. All sorts of extra things have to be bought for him, and that can't happen if there's a reduction in income.'

'I agree with you and I hope that all countries will, sooner or later, follow your example. Are there any spectacular benefits about which you think I should know?'

'Yes. Comrade Stalin taught the importance of the family. That is why we look after our mothers and children. All possible assistance is given to a pregnant woman. We give her a maternity grant, and take care of her during her confinement.'

'I am glad to know it. What astonishes me is your assumption that yours is the only country in the world which does these things. It so happens that a man called Jesus had something to say about family life long before Comrade Stalin was ever thought of; and as for maternity grants and benefits for expectant mothers, we have all those things in England.'

'That's propaganda. You are just a spokesman of the Churchill Tory Government.'

'Really! There is a limit to the insults that can be poured on a man! But how do you know we don't have these things and that I'm just telling you a fairy story?'

'We read the *Daily Worker*.'

'But surely you don't believe what you read in the *Daily Worker*?'

'Why not?'

'It's written by Communists.'

They appreciated the point and amid the laughter I turned to the question of retirement.

'At what age do most people stop going to work?'

'Fifty-five.'

'That seems rather early. In England it's sixty, or sixty-five; in fact a lot of people are still in harness until they are seventy.'

'But we are a Communist country and we don't drive our old people until they drop dead. When they are old and tired we let them retire and enjoy their rest.'

'Perhaps, my friends, it's just because we don't drive our workers that most people in my country feel neither old nor tired at fifty-five. If what I am told about Soviet conditions is true I'm not the least surprised that your people are finished in early middle-age and die before we do. In Britain thousands of people are still immensely vigorous at seventy and strongly resent the suggestion they should sit back and do nothing. But we won't have a political argument about that. Tell me, what's the average working week?'

'Forty-eight hours.'

'Does that allow for one day off?'

'Yes. We work eight hours on six days.'

'That means there's no half day?'

'No.'

'That's interesting. In England we never work on Saturday afternoons: in fact lots of workers have the whole day free.'

'We know. But that is a capitalist dodge to keep down unemployment. By not allowing the workers to work on Saturday the employers save a day's wages and jobs take longer to finish, and the shortage of work is less apparent.'

'That's most interesting as it shows the lengths to which political neurosis can go. It is the old case of "heads I win, tails you lose". If we give our workers leisure to enjoy themselves, it is to keep the capitalists in power; if we don't we are at our old game of grinding the faces of the poor! But leaving all that on one side, what about overtime and Sunday work?'

'We avoid it if we can and it doesn't often happen. With wise planning there's no need for it except in an emergency.'

'I'm glad to hear you say that. I wish we had the sense to realize this in England. Unfortunately some workers deliberately look for a trade which makes a practice of overtime and I am sure that much of it is quite unnecessary, besides being very wasteful.'

Next I brought up the question of absenteeism. My hosts were not anxious to discuss discipline because they wanted me to suppose, just as the headmaster of school No. 315 did, that in the Soviet State people automatically do the right thing.

'You told me just now that there's no half day on Saturdays. What happens if a worker goes to football instead of reporting to the factory?'

'Games are held on Sunday afternoons and weekday evenings, so he couldn't go.'

'Suppose then he went to the films?'

'If he did, and it isn't very likely, he would be verbally reprimanded and, if necessary, the reprimand would be repeated in writing.'

'And if that didn't do the trick?'

'He would appear before a committee of his workmates whose job it would be to make him realize the seriousness of his offence. And his name would probably be posted on the factory wall-paper.'

'Is that the extreme penalty?'

'No. If he is really awkward and won't work properly he will either be reduced to a less favourable position or he will be dismissed. But we must make it clear he has the right to appeal throughout these proceedings and his case will come before an impartial tribunal. But these sort of things don't happen often, as slackness is regarded as anti-social and public opinion is against it.'

I wish it had been possible to check this. As it was I had no real means of checking production figures. Of course there are propaganda statistics, but they are not reliable. Nevertheless, whatever the reasons may be, men seemed to work hard. I remember watching a gang of roadmenders on the outskirts of Moscow. They worked with a will and the least sign of loitering was noticed by the foreman and reprimanded. How different from this country. A week or two ago I motored from Bristol to Wells and the road was up in three places; and the one thing common to each was the number of men hanging around gossiping. On the day before I left Russia I spent half an hour in the Red Square outside a store which was in the process of construction. Women worked furiously with pneumatic drills, and hastened up ladders with hods, while the bricklayers and plasterers never wasted a moment.

Perhaps one strong reason for working hard is the fear of exposure. The *Moscow Evening News* is a mine of domestic information. A man, for example, goes to a store and buys a pair of shoes which are faulty and let in the water. He sends a letter to the paper demanding an explanation. There is an investigation. If the complaint is justified, the manager of the boot factory will make a grovelling apology and either he or the operatives more immediately concerned will be punished. Again, a Muscovite goes into the country for a picnic. The conductor on the bus is rude to him and the tea at the restaurant is not worth drinking. Off goes the letter to the *Moscow Evening News*. The driver and the proprietor are both mentioned and in all probability a confession will follow. It would seem that in a capitalist society a manufacturer, if he wants to remain in business, has to depend upon a standard of quality to attract the interest of the customer, whereas in a Communist one, where there is no competition and a man's bank balance does not depend upon his commercial enterprise, he is kept up to the mark by the threat of denunciation. I dislike the Russian method because I loathe snooping, both for itself and because of the opportunities it gives to mean-minded gossips and intrigues, but I realize there is a problem to be solved. As the years go by, more and more industries are bound to be nationalized. If men feel no personal responsibility and they know that, no matter how idle they are, their wages will be unaffected, what is to be done? Even now I could fill up an entire edition of an *Evening News!*

I had read a lot about the Stakhanovite movement but I was not clear how it differed from the 'speed-up' which is roundly condemned by our trade unionists. As a result of my conversations at the Institute of Labour my doubts are dispersed. There is no difference.

The constitution says that it is the duty of the trade unions 'To organize the socialist emulation of workers and other employees for fulfilling and exceeding State plans, raising labour productivity, improving quality and reducing production costs; take part in planning and regulating wages and in framing systems of pay in accordance with the socialist system of payment by the amount and quality of work performed; promote the introduction of new progressive output standards and see that correct records are made of work done and the piece-rate, and progressive bonus system of payment is correctly operated.'

I hope readers will have another look at this quotation. If it had been produced at an 'Any Questions' programme, I suspect the team would have attributed it to an eighteenth-century Tory manifesto! Human beings are odd creatures. If you tell them they are being exploited, they get hot under the collar; if you call them Stakhanovites, they are flattered.

It may be that the 'speed-up' is legitimate—it certainly would do some British workers a power of good—but it is sheer humbug to pretend that the Russian Stakhanovite system is different. It is a cleverly devised method to stimulate production and to eliminate slackness.

'I want to learn all about Stakhanovites,' I said. 'Give me a few examples so that I can understand how the system works.'

The manager fetched a poster, dated 1950, of a team of bricklayers who had been specially complimented by Stalin and given a large monetary reward. I had seen this poster in public places so I was glad of the opportunity to have it explained to me.

'The ordinary bricklayer,' he said, 'lays 2,500 bricks a day, but the Stakhanovite lays many more, perhaps 5,000. In 1950, as this poster shows, Comrade Stalin praised these men because, between them, they were responsible for 253,600 bricks in a single day.'

'How is the team made up?'

'Twelve bricklayers, twelve assistants, twelve bringer men —thirty-six in all.'

'I find this almost impossible to believe.'

'Why? How many bricks does the British labourer lay?'

'About five or six hundred.'

'An hour?'

'No, a day.'

They roared with laughter and asked me to give a serious answer. And I had a similar experience when I visited a building exhibition and talked with some operatives. One of them said: 'But that is ridiculous. A man could lay five hundred bricks with his eyes shut.'

'Be that as it may,' I continued, 'I suspect your way of laying bricks is different from ours.'

'Our men usually lay five at a time.' And they showed me the gadget for doing this. 'Don't your men do the same? If not, why not?'

'Perhaps the wicked capitalists won't let them for fear they may finish their jobs too quickly! But let's get back to the Stakhanovites. If this poster is true and, in fairness, I must tell you I don't believe it, the results have been achieved by sweated labour.'

'That isn't so. These men, filled with a desire to serve their Soviet homeland, thought out new ways for improving production. In your country the profits from increased labour go to the private owners; here they benefit the men themselves.'

'That is largely nonsense, because increased profits are heavily taxed. In any case some industries, coal mining for instance, have been nationalized and no profits go to private people. I must say I should love to know what the British miner would say to his Stakhanovite comrade if, as a result of his presence in their midst, production had to be increased by thirty per cent.'

'I don't think, Canon Stockwood, you understand the difficulties which faced our Government after the Revolution. The workers were illiterate and untrained. Comrade Lenin and Comrade Stalin had a tremendous task. They had to industrialize a great country, build factories, dams, roads, electrical plant. We could not dawdle. So Comrade Stalin decided to honour the workers who took the initiative and set an example to their fellows. The result is that people are always producing more because they think out better methods and work harder.'

'I appreciate the problem and I think it may be right, in some circumstances, to let the special effort of the individual worker become the norm for everybody. But that doesn't alter the fact that, once you have stripped the Stakhanovite movement of its Communist jargon, it's the old system of bonuses and piece wages. To put it vulgarly, so that your worker can get a tolerable wage he has to sweat his guts. And as soon as he has shown that production can be improved by a quarter, the addition becomes part of the norm. That is something the trade unions in Britain have fought for years. It's possible, for instance, that five hundred bricks a day are too few and the number should be increased to a thousand. I am sure it could be done and perhaps it ought to be the norm. And it might be that a few enthusiasts could manage twice that number, but it would be altogether wrong to look upon them as average.'

'We come back to the real test. You have the right to expect a man to give his best when the country belongs to him, but when it is owned by capitalists he must protect himself.'

'I'm afraid that is beyond my understanding, but as you rightly say I am a *bourgeois* clergyman; so you must not expect me to follow the argument. Tell me, what are the rates of pay for a factory Stakhanovite, and what other benefits does he get?'

'The average factory worker gets about £5 a week. If he is a skilled man he may get £10, especially if he is on essential work. The Stakhanovite can reach £15, or in some cases £20. Usually it is about twice the ordinary level. But that isn't all. He and his family will have a free holiday, perhaps in the Crimea, and there are special privileges at the factory. Of course if there are several Stakhanovites in a particular works the whole group will benefit. If you look at those photographs on the wall, you will see that trees and grass plots have been planted so that the Stakhanovites can rest in the shade during the dinner break. And at that factory is a fountain and a swimming-pool. And here's a factory with a great many improvements—dormitories for the men, a kindergarten for the children, a library and a theatre. In time all Soviet factories will have these amenities, but it's up to the workers themselves to strive for them. That is why the Stakhanovite has such an important part to play. He is in the advance guard. He knows that the chief thing about his labour is not his monthly wage but his contribution toward creating a Communist society. And he knows that he must help the other workers to have a fresh outlook as Soviet citizens. They must learn to improve conditions, and improve themselves.'

'And how do the Stakhanovites set about educating their comrades?'

'In many factories there are schools for workers. Meetings are held frequently at which improvements are discussed and policy is explained. Always the Stakhanovite points to the Soviet goal, so that the workers feel a pride in helping to reach it.'

'Do you think it's pride in the goal which makes them work hard, or financial reward? If a Stakhanovite gets twice as much as his neighbour and if he is given decent housing conditions, a flat of his own with a bathroom, it's not surprising that he gets on with his job. I don't doubt there are some who are altruistic in their approach. You get that in every sort of society. A few men, for some reason or another, are more interested in their work than in their rewards and they will do much more than is required of them. But the majority are indifferent about philosophical and political goals. They look upon work as a necessary evil and their real interest is the wage packet. I know we need a completely new attitude toward work in England. You, of course, think the fault is capitalism. It may be a contributing factor, but it's only one. There's so much hanging around and messing about. I often think we could almost double production if we didn't fritter away so much time on tea breaks.'

'What are tea breaks?'

'Surely you know? Interruptions in the day's work for making tea, drinking it and having a gossip.'

'Such things are unknown in the Soviet Union. The workers have good meals in the canteens at the proper times, but we do not allow eating and drinking at other times.'

'I'm interested to learn this and I hope you will pass this information to the Dean of Canterbury when he next visits you and he can write a special article about it in the *Daily Worker*. I can see the headline "Moscow closes down on tea breaks. Stakhanovite Malenkov suggests London should do the same."'

'Our people do not want to be idle. They know the standard of living is being raised by their own efforts. Every month there are new factories, more houses, more goods in the shops. Already this year there have been three big price cuts. They remember the dreadful life they used to have; that is why they are keen to build a better future.'

It is doubtful whether more than a few remember the past, as most of the workers of today would have been children then, if they had been born. But there is no doubt that skilful propaganda has made them aware of the changes. They know what conditions used to be; they know what they are; they know what they are intended to become.

Not all propaganda is bad and it's a pity we don't teach our own people what remarkable changes have been achieved in Britain during the past fifty years. I sometimes show photographs to my young parishioners of my parish as it used to be at the beginning of the century—horrible slums, queues of unemployed, shabby clothes, pinched faces—and they are always astonished. And I tell them that the job has only been half done and it's up to them to finish it off. In this way they begin to take the right sort of pride in their country.

Before we leave Stakhanovites I must quote one paragraph from page twenty-six of the constitution because I know Communist critics will accuse me of misrepresenting the movement and insisting that it has nothing to do with the 'speed-up'. 'It is the duty of a trade union to establish Stakhanovite schools and arrange for assistance to novices by experienced workers, engineers, and technicians; to arrange talks and lectures on efficient methods of work, and help the personnel in other ways to fulfil and exceed their output quotas and improve their skill.'

I asked my hosts how a boy set about getting a job in the Soviet Union and was informed that the Government stated its needs and the trade unions advertised the vacancies. Advertisements are also put on boards at street corners. I told them I thought the British way was better.

'We have Youth Employment Officers who visit the schools during the boys' last term. They talk over matters with the headmaster, the parents and the boys before suggesting a vacancy. The officers keep in touch with him and, if things don't work out happily, something else is tried.'

'I am afraid, Canon Stockwood, you are once more being the Tory spokesman!'

'What makes you think that?'

'We know your Government does not care for the workers. Even if it did, the scheme would be pointless.'

'Why?'

'Because in England there are millions of unemployed, and it is stupid for an officer to interview a boy when he knows he cannot get him a job.'

'My friends, do you really believe this drivel? I know your knowledge of Britain is based upon what you read in the *Daily*

Worker and learn from Communist delegations. Both delight
to damn their own country and to paint it in the worst
possible colours, but there's a limit to their lying.'

'We know this from our comrades and we have to choose
whether to believe them or you. You are not a worker and it
is not in your interests to support the unemployed.'

'In that case why do you not come to England and see for
yourself? If you are so certain everything is bad, then what
you say about the appalling conditions in a Western State will
be confirmed and you will be able to return to the Soviet
Union and tell your comrades how lucky they are.'

'We do not need to see for ourselves; we know. It is not
just the *Daily Worker* which tells us the truth. Our own
sailors when they returned from the coronation of Queen
Elizabeth reported in the newspapers and on the radio the
terrible misery of the workers in England. They wandered
around London and saw children, with practically no clothes
on, collapsing in the streets through starvation.'

'I repeat the challenge. Come and see. And if you come,
don't let the Soviet Embassy or the *Daily Worker* take you for
bogus trips to Bethnal Green, but look at English life as a
whole, the good with the bad. The real tragedy is, of course,
you would never be allowed to come on those conditions and
you dare not ask. Marxism is based on a number of supersti-
tions, and everything must be made to fit. If you should see
anything which might cause you to question those supersti-
tions, then you must not be allowed to see it. And the fact is,
British democracy drives a coach and four through the out-
dated speculations of Karl Marx.'

We were back to politics and, as time was getting short, I
thought we should conclude on a non-controversial note. So I
asked for information.

'I've learnt a lot this afternoon, and have a fairly good idea
of wage scales, but will you complete the picture by saying
something about taxation?'

'Income tax varies between seven and ten per cent. That is the main tax.'

'Anything else?'

'Yes, one that wouldn't be popular with you—a bachelor's tax! Rather, people without children, whether single or married, pay extra taxes.'

'That seems fair enough. What about family allowances?'

'If a man has less than £3 a week he gets an allowance.'

'I am surprised your income tax is so low. In England, after an initial tax-free allowance, it's roughly fifty per cent and it works up to ninety-five per cent.'

'If that is true, how is it that hundreds of your rich land-lords live in castles?'

'In fact most of the castles and the landlords are in ruins! But I am not going to start another political argument. I must be content with the statement of a fact. Your rich men are better off than ours, because their taxes are infinitely less. Now before you contradict that, let me pass quickly to another question. If a worker has surplus money what can he do with it?'

'He can invest it in State securities.'

'What is the interest?'

'Three per cent.'

'And suppose the money accumulates, what happens when he dies?'

'He leaves it to his relatives.'

'Can he leave anything else?'

'Yes, whatever he likes—his goods, property and house.'

'But I had not realized that a man can own his own house in a Soviet State. I thought they all belonged to the Govern-ment.'

'No. If he can afford to buy a house, he can do what he likes with it.'

This I found most interesting and significant. Sooner or later a middle class is bound to emerge. A man has a good

income, perhaps £2,500 p.a. He owns a house on the outskirts
of Moscow and has a small investment. His one child is
a boy. Unlike most of his contemporaries who live in over-
crowded rooms, he has the benefit of a cultured home, and
a study in which to work. The chances are he will do well at
school, go to the university and land a lucrative job. As he
approaches middle age his father dies and leaves everything
to him. By this time he is married and has a small family of his
own. Inevitably he will associate with people who have similar
standards and his children will become friendly with and
eventually find partners in the same set. To some extent this
has, I think, already happened. I asked one of my guides to
what extent there were class differences in Russia.

'There have been none since the Revolution.'

'That is the Marxist answer, but I want the truth. Tell
me honestly, what would your reaction be if a son of yours were
to marry a girl who swept the roads?'

'I shouldn't like it. It is usually best for people to set up
homes with partners who have the same interests and
educational appreciations.'

'I agree, but it hardly squares with your classless society,
because you are indirectly admitting that there is, and must
be, an intelligentsia, and that the intelligentsia is likely to
reproduce itself.'

That brought my visit to the Institute of Labour, Moscow's
Transport House, to an end. There had been hard hitting,
but we parted agreeably and I think both sides had enjoyed
themselves. As a parting shot I was showered with leaflets.
I brought them back with me to England and one of them
lies open on my desk as I write. Here is a paragraph on wage
differentials: 'Marxism has never recognized and does not
recognize any kind of equality. Marxism is based on the fact
that human tastes and human needs are not, and cannot be,
identical or equal in quality or quantity, either in the socialist
or in the communist period. To aver that socialism calls for

a levelling, an equalization, of the needs of the members of society, a levelling of their tastes and their personal existences, to aver that according to the plans of the Marxists all men must wear the same suits and eat the same dishes, in identical quantities, that would be to proclaim inanities and to slander Marxism.'

These words were penned by Comrade Stalin.

Appendix to Chapter 5

FOOD

	£	s.	d.	
Bread, black			4	lb.
best quality			10	,,
Flour		1	1½	,,
Pastries		5	0	,,
Beef		3	3	,,
Mutton		3	9	,,
Pork		9	3	,,
Canned meat		5	3	,,
Tinned crab		3	2	a tin
Sausages		3	4	lb.
Tinned salmon		4	4	a tin
Chicken		4	5	lb.
Goose		3	0	,,
Turkey		5	0	,,
Bacon		8	0	,,
Ham		7	9	,,
Cod		2	7	,,
Herring		4	3	,,
Salmon		15	0	,,
Black Caviare	1	5	0	,,
Red Caviare		12	0	,,
Butter		7	0	,,
Margarine		3	8	,,
Cheese		9	0	,,
Eggs			6	each
Tea	1	5	0	lb.
Sugar		2	6	,,
Potatoes			4	,,

	£	s.	d.	
Tomatoes		7	6	lb.
Carrots		1	0	,,
Onions			9	,,
Lettuce		2	6	,,
Apples		1	6	,,
Oranges		1	0	each
Nuts		3	6	lb.
Rice		2	2	,,
Cocoa	1	7	6	,,
Chocolate, cheap		15	0	,,
best	2	2	0	,,
Sweets		9	0	,,
Coffee		10	1	,,
Jam		2	7	,,
Champagne		11	0	a bottle

CLOTHING

Men

	£	s.	d.
Two-piece suit, minimum	15	7	0
average	25	0	0
expensive	40	0	0
Overcoat	21	14	0
Flannel trousers	10	0	0
Raincoat	5	5	6
Felt hat	2	0	0
Fur hat	4	0	0
Cap		17	6
Bathing trunks		8	6
Tie		10	6
Silk handkerchief		9	0
Shirt, minimum	1	12	6
expensive	3	0	0
Vest		7	4
Pants		6	3
Socks		5	8
Pyjamas, minimum	2	18	6
expensive	12	18	6
Shoes, minimum	1	14	6
expensive	12	0	0
Wellingtons	2	18	0
Football boots	3	7	6

Women

		£	s.	d.
Costume, minimum	. . . . .	10	14	6
expensive	. . . . .	21	0	0
Blouse, rayon	. . . . .	2	11	0
silk	. . . . .	4	5	0
Overcoat, winter	. . . . .	15	8	0
summer	. . . . .	13	18	6
Raincoat	. . . . .	6	19	6
Felt hat, minimum	. . . . .		18	1
expensive	. . . . .	2	5	8
Gloves	. . . . .		12	7
Bathing costume	. . . . .		17	0
Slip	. . . . .		19	11
Knickers	. . . . .		12	6
Nightgown	. . . . .	1	11	9
Corsets	. . . . .	3	7	0
Stockings, minimum	. . . . .		4	6
expensive	. . . . .	1	0	0
Nylon stockings	. . . . .		17	0
Pyjamas, silk	. . . . .	12	18	6
rayon	. . . . .	4	16	0
Brassière	. . . . .		6	0
Outdoor shoes, minimum	. . . .	6	1	6
expensive	. . . .	7	17	6
Indoor shoes	. . . . .	2	0	0
Plimsolls	. . . . .		11	11

Children

Two-piece suit	. . . . .	10	0	0
Raincoat	. . . . .	5	17	0
Overcoat	. . . . .	6	7	0
Pullover	. . . . .	1	1	6
School frock	. . . . .	2	5	6
Woollen dress	. . . . .	5	0	0
Cotton dress	. . . . .	2	10	0
Boy's shirt	. . . . .		17	3
Boy's vest	. . . . .		11	6
Pyjamas	. . . . .		8	1

HOUSEHOLD GOODS AND MISCELLANEOUS

	£	s.	d.
Bedstead, steel	6	15	0
wooden with mattress . .	25	11	0
Chair, minimum	2	2	6
expensive	4	3	0
Wardrobe	28	10	0
Upholstered chair	20	6	0
Table	7	1	0
Kitchen cupboard	10	4	0
Piano, grand	300	0	0
upright	150	0	0
Bedroom suite	172	17	0
Radio set, minimum	4	10	0
average	16	5	0
expensive	32	10	0
Television set, minimum . . .	30	0	0
average	59	10	0
expensive	206	0	0
Gramophone	8	5	0
Gramophone record		1	7
long-playing record . .		2	6
Tennis racquet	4	8	6
Alarm clock		14	7
Wrist-watch, minimum . . .	6	0	0
expensive	31	12	6
Pocket watch	5	13	6
Bicycle	12	13	0
Motor cycle	57	7	6
Motor car, Moskvich	400	0	0
Pobeda	800	0	0
Zim	1,350	0	0
Zis	4,000	0	0
Vacuum cleaner	11	5	0
Refrigerator, minimum . . .	17	0	0
expensive	50	0	0
Washing machine	15	0	0
Cup and saucer		3	8
Tumbler		1	8
Knife		2	4
Fork		1	6
Toothbrush		1	0
Hairbrush		9	0

	£	s.	d.
Lipstick		1	10
Fountain pen		11	9
Theatre ticket, minimum . . .		2	6
expensive		17	6
Cinema ticket, minimum . . .		1	6
expensive		3	0
Football stadium		1	0
Man's haircut		1	0
Woman's permanent wave		13	9
Average meal in restaurant		12	6
Twenty cigarettes, minimum . . .		1	6
expensive . . .		3	1

WEEKLY WAGES

	£	s.	d.
President of university	93	15	0
Senior university professor	62	10	0
Senior ecclesiastic	52	0	0
Medical consultant	42	10	0
Head of library	25	0	0
Junior university don	15	10	0
Superintendent of clinic	12	10	0
Head of planning department of a Moscow administration	12	10	0
Senior book-keeper in a Moscow administration	10	0	0
Engineer with diploma	9	10	0
Senior superintendent of work . . .	9	0	0
Engineer-electrician	8	0	0
Junior doctor	7	10	0
Senior nurse	6	5	0
Senior engineer	6	5	0
Book-keeper-inspector	6	0	0
Senior library official	5	15	0
Civil servants (average wage) . . .	5	10	0
Building workers ⎱		From	
Turners ⎰ according to . .	4	7	6
Fitters ⎱ piece work		to	
Moulders ⎰	8	0	0
Electrical switchboard technicians . .	5	0	0
Box maker	4	7	6
Chauffeur	4	0	0

WORKERS' PARADISE

		£	s.	d.
Typist	. . . .	3	15	0
Fitters	. . . . . .	3	15	0
Junior nurse	. . . . .	3	15	0
Bus conductor	. . . . .	3	12	6
Road mender	. . . . .	5	0	0
Kindergarten teacher	. . .	3	15	0
Floor polisher	. . . . .	3	2	6
Cashier	. . . . . .	3	2	6
Stock-keeper	. . . . .	2	15	6
Lift operator	. . . . .	2	12	0
Watchman	. . . . .	2	12	0
Woman messenger	. . .	2	5	0
Cook	. . . . . .	2	5	0
Unskilled factory worker—minimum	. .	2	0	0
	maximum	3	5	0

Chapter Six

FARMS, FACTORIES, AND RED TAPE

BEFORE I left England, the Archbishop of Canterbury's
chaplain for Foreign Relations, Mr H. M. Waddams,
recommended a visit to Zagorsk monastery, a famous
shrine in the annals of Russian Christianity. Soon after my
arrival I told Intourist I wanted to go and I was informed that
inquiries would be made.

'I am sorry, Canon Stockwood, but it is not possible to
arrange the visit,' said the director at the National.

'Why?'

'It is a long way. The car would be expensive. And I do
not think you would be able to go around the most interesting
buildings.'

I expressed my regrets and at once determined to find
another way for getting to Zagorsk. An opportunity soon
came. That afternoon I had to call at the British Embassy
and a member of the staff, Peter Mennell, kindly suggested
he would take me for a trip in his car on the following Saturday. 'Is there anywhere special you would like to go?' he
asked.

'Yes, Zagorsk monastery.'

'We can easily fix that. I'll send a car to the National to
bring you to my flat at 9.30 and then you and James Bennett
can transfer to my car and we'll make a day of it.'

As was my custom I told Intourist what had happened. I
knew the authorities were bound to discover sooner or later
and, in any case, I made up my mind before reaching the

Summer home at Otdyk for children of Moscow workers

The Bolshoi Theatre, home of Russian ballet

The Kremlin

U.S.S.R. that there should be nothing secret about my movements.

'Mr Rogov, everything's fixed about Zagorsk,' I said. 'There's no need to bother about a car. I'm going with some of the people at the Embassy. So don't book anything for Saturday as I shall be away all day.'

'That is very interesting. I hope you have a nice day.'

What happened when he passed the information on to his superior officer I don't know, but I imagine somebody must have been called over the coals. Next day it was made clear to me that the proposed trip was not popular.

'Canon Stockwood, there is no need for the British Embassy to take you to Zagorsk, as I now find we can arrange it.'

'I'm sorry, Mr Rogov, but I have accepted the invitation and it would be discourteous to decline.'

'But while you are in Moscow, Intourist is your host, and Intourist takes pleasure in looking after you.'

'That's very kind, but it really is too late. What is more, although Intourist is my host, it makes me pay for hiring cars and, because of the rate of exchange, the charges are prohibitive. Why, a trip to Zagorsk would cost me thirty pounds!'

That was not the end. A few hours later Mr Rogov, one of the kindliest and most courteous men on earth, returned to the attack.

'I have taken up the matter of the cost, Canon Stockwood, and I am pleased to tell you there will be no charge. As you are anxious to see Zagorsk monastery we will provide a car free.'

'I'm sorry, but as I explained this morning, I have accepted the invitation to go with my English friends.'

That was by no means the end. On the Thursday evening, a few hours after I had returned from my interview with the Patriarch, Mr Rogov told me it was inconvenient to visit Zagorsk on a Saturday and he suggested Friday as an alternative.

'Mr Rogov,' I said, 'why don't you want me to go with the British? First of all, you tell me Intourist can't fix a trip to Zagorsk and then, when the Embassy comes to the rescue, you fall over yourselves to take me.'

'You misunderstand me, Canon Stockwood. We are anxious to please. Saturday is not a good day for the monastery. If you go then, you can only see a few things. If you come with us tomorrow, you can see everything and the church officials will show you over.'

'That is curious, Mr Rogov, because I happened to mention the visit to the Patriarch this morning, and he said the monastery would be pleased to welcome me on Saturday. It's true he added that many of the monks and theological students would be observing a rule of silence, but that won't seriously affect our plans.'

Poor Mr Rogov! He didn't know what to say. On Friday he made a final effort. 'I suggest you come in our car with the guide and you can meet your friends at Zagorsk. We can supply food for all of you.'

'Really, Mr Rogov, that is an odd proposition! I accept the hospitality of my British friends and now I am to tell them I will go in another car but produce the refreshments. That is not our way of doing things in England and I'm afraid I cannot accede to your request.'

I still don't know what was the cause of this manœuvre. It's possible it was nothing more sinister than the creaking of the bureaucratic machine. Perhaps the officials had imagined I intended to spend the whole time in Moscow and had made no provision for outside excursions and, when I confronted Mr Rogov with my request, he did not feel able to authorize a departure from the schedule. May be that is why he refused in the first instance. But when it became clear I was going with Embassy officials, the schedule was quickly revised as it was feared I might learn too much. No doubt I was an embarrassing guest. Most foreigners, being Communists or 'fellow-travellers', keep as far away from their embassies as possible. That suits the Soviet book, because it's thought that diplomats have too much prejudiced information with which to poison the minds of visitors. The fact is, efforts were made on several occasions to hinder meetings and meals with the English-speaking embassies.

My host on the Zagorsk trip, Peter Mennell, was as fair-minded as a man could be. He gave me facts and statistics in plenty, but rarely expressed personal opinions unless I asked for them. But perhaps Intourist distrusts facts and statistics which lack the Soviet imprimatur, for fear they may contradict the official propaganda.

The drive to Zagorsk was uneventful except that it took me through several towns and villages and gave me a chance to see conditions as they really were. The roads were very different from the broad thoroughfares in Moscow. Some were up to Western standards, but often we found ourselves on rubble and mud. We dropped into one or two churches and found the priests conducting a Saturday morning service for the peasants, most of whom were elderly women, as the younger folk were at work.

I was especially interested in a road repair squad. There seemed to be as many women as men and once again I watched a woman handling a pneumatic drill. I couldn't make out whether these workers were employed freely or were the inmates of a prison labour camp.

The villages were not attractive. Most of the houses were ugly wooden structures, crying out for a coat of paint. Sanitation was almost non-existent. A day or two later when I walked through a hamlet with the Ambassador to view an old church, we watched the peasants washing their clothes in the stream and fetching water from the one tap in the mud street.

Zagorsk itself is immensely impressive. The great walled monastery with its magnificent cathedrals overshadows the nondescript town. As we had time to spare we had lunch at a restaurant, the best of its kind. The food was good and the tables clean. The caviare was admirable and the wine adequate. But there was an unpleasant snag. An army officer, sitting in a velvet-draped box, had done himself too well on vodka and was being disgustingly sick. The waitress released a curtain to screen him from view, but the sound of retching punctuated our meal and the smell was not helpful, though I did my best to drown it with the excellent coffee.

When we had finished I moved toward the toilet, but after I had taken one look, I quickly retreated. I have encountered squalid sanitation in my own city, especially in the slums, but I've never witnessed anything quite so grim as Zagorsk. Peter Mennell, whose experience is considerably greater than mine, assured me that the accommodation was well above average. I take his word for it, though I find it difficult to believe that anything could be worse, or more revolting. I wonder if Intourist volunteered to supply a picnic lunch in the hope of keeping me away from the restaurant lavatory. Mr Rogov knew that as chairman of the health committee of Bristol City Council I was interested in public health matters and had on several occasions commented on sanitary arrangements. He knew that I had severely criticized the conveniences in Moscow, but they were Utopian as compared with their counterparts at Zagorsk.

Canon Sergei, an official of the monastery, awaited us at the entrance. With him were two laymen who had come from Moscow to act as guides—Mr Bulevsky, an authority on architecture, and Dr Dochtusov, a lecturer at the theological academy. From their conversation and gestures they seemed to be devout members of the Orthodox Church and they could not have been more helpful. At the same time they were excellent propagandists for the Soviet régime and I wondered if they had been chosen to act as guides because of their political reliability.

As soon as we had exchanged greetings Dr Dochtusov took Canon Sergei aside and asked him if he had turned away the beggars from the porch of the cathedral. I was not supposed to hear this, but the conversation wasn't lost upon James Bennett who understood the language. Canon Sergei hurried off and the beggars had disappeared by the time we reached the church. I was, therefore, interested to learn from another member of the Embassy staff, who visited Zagorsk on the following day, that the porch was filled with elderly people asking alms.

The cathedral, a comparatively small building, is held in special veneration and the services are continuous. Apparently the clergy operate in relays throughout the day. A priest was chanting on the chancel steps and a congregation of sixty or seventy joined in the responses. To a Westerner it seemed mechanical and dreary, but one has to remember that the Orthodox Church has a deep sense of the timelessness of the liturgy. It is the business of the Church to fix the minds of the faithful on the majesty of God and brief, popular services are not encouraged.

As I was looking at an icon on the chancel screen the priest stopped the service for a few moments to greet me. The informality was charming. It always happened. Although we belonged to different traditions and spoke with different tongues, we shared a common priesthood.

Canon Sergei took us to the Patriarch's palace. It was magnificent. I am sure there would be ructions in the Church of England if the Archbishop of Canterbury lived in such grandeur. Beautiful rooms, with lovely furniture and splendid carpets and an enchanting roof garden. And yet there was a curious austerity. The Patriarch's bedroom was simple and his study, where he spends the greater part of his time when in residence, was severely furnished. The private chapel was impressive, partly because of its decoration, but more so because it gave the impression of being used.

Canon Sergei told me that the Patriarch looked upon his palace as a retreat. He did not have much time to visit it, perhaps four times a year. When he came he devoted the time to prayer and writing books. We were taken to the conference room where the bishops assemble, and when I asked if I might ask questions on the general position of the Church in the Soviet Union, I was placed in the Patriarch's chair at the head of the table. We talked frankly, but Dr Dochtusov gave nothing away in his replies. He avoided criticisms of the régime and tried to convince me that the Orthodox Church was free to go its way. I put forward the points which trouble most Westerners, but I was told that whatever the difficulties may have been, most of them had been removed. Dr Dochtusov added that, although atheistic materialism was an embarrassment, the Government had done much to raise the standards of the people and the Church should be grateful.

From the Patriarch's palace we went to the two larger cathedrals which are being restored, and I was introduced to the monk who was responsible for the work. He was an erudite craftsman and an accomplished artist. As far as I could make out the buildings had fallen into disuse and had only recently been handed back to the Church.

The bells chimed for service and the theological students and the monks started to arrive. Dr Dochtusov said they numbered about three hundred. Unfortunately it was beginning to get dark and we had to return to Moscow. As we left, we dropped into a small tumble-down chapel which was packed. The priest, an elderly peasant, asked Canon Sergei to introduce me and, placing both arms on my shoulders, gave me the kiss of peace. The congregation did not seem in the least surprised at this interruption, but bowed their heads for my blessing. It was a strangely moving epilogue to my visit to Zagorsk.

During my first week in Moscow *Pravda* and the radio gave

publicity to a damning indictment of Soviet agriculture by Mr Khruschev, the first secretary of the Communist Party. In his diatribe against Russian farmers he said there were more cattle in the U.S.S.R. in 1916 than in 1953. This surprised me because I had been given to understand that the agrarian revolution, although ruthless, had been efficient. I immediately asked Mr Rogov if he would make it possible for me to visit a collective farm. I repeated my request each day, but without avail. The answer varied: 'It is too difficult to arrange'; 'There is not a suitable farm in the Moscow region'; 'We should be pleased to fix it at another time, but it is the wrong time of year'; 'The journey is a long one and the taxi would be too expensive.' I did my best to overcome the opposition. 'Mr Rogov, don't you realize that the British are interested in your agricultural experiments? If they are successful you should be proud to show me. I shall be asked lots of questions when I return to England and I want to have first-hand evidence.' But I always encountered a Molotov negative.

Again, I don't know whether the refusal was due to bureaucratic red-tape or to deliberate design. I suspect the former. The schedule of visits had been approved before my arrival and it did not include a collective farm. To get the schedule altered demanded a hundred-and-one imprimaturs and poor Mr Rogov could not take the responsibility upon himself.

An American, who was staying at my hotel, had asked to inspect a farm before his arrival. Permission was granted. In fact he was allowed to take his camera with him and he came home with several useful photographs. He was less sympathetic to the Soviet régime than I was and more outspoken in his criticisms. That is one reason why I am inclined to think that the treatment accorded to me was due to nothing more sinister than top-heavy officialdom. If I had been wise enough to ask before I had left England, Intourist would have collected the requisite number of approving signatures and all would have been well. But, thanks to my American friend, I learnt a lot and his information was supplemented by talks at the embassies.

The Russian mujik, or peasant, has never been renowned for hard work. Illiteracy, superstition, drunkenness and sloth have contributed to his downfall. The results were disastrous and the harvest often failed through his incompetence. When the Soviets came to power the position grew worse. Naturally conservative and suspicious, the mujik resisted tendencies toward collectivization. He knew that the new economic policy was based upon the abolition of private ownership and he feared, not without reason, for the future of his holding.

The Government was compelled to take stern measures. It was useless to embark upon plans to industrialize the country, unless the populations in the cities could be fed. Propaganda and persuasion were ineffective, so other methods had to be devised to overcome individualism and primitive conditions. Grain and animals were confiscated and the farmers were ordered to surrender a large proportion of their produce. The farmers resisted, either by killing their animals and eating them themselves, or refusing to work. So Stalin declared war. Agriculture was put on the same footing as industry. All the means of production were seized by the Government and, common ownership having been established, the authorities determined how the land was to be distributed. The Kolkhosi, or collective farms, run into thousands and millions of peasants are involved. A few individual farmers still exist, but the number is negligible, whereas in pre-revolutionary days there were twenty-five million small holdings.

The collective farm is supposed to be a partnership of peasant-farmers who have pooled their lands, their animals and their implements. It has a measure of autonomy, but its programme is necessarily determined by the fact that each year it has to sell to the Government a large proportion of its produce. The amount it receives is well below the ordinary market price, but the difference is regarded as rent. What it has over and above the amount demanded by the authorities can be disposed of as it pleases. Some is kept for private use, but much is sold for a good price in the open market. I visited several markets in the streets of Moscow. There were dozens of stalls and they were thronged with people. I have often seen their counterparts in England, but there is a difference. In our country the market is usually cheaper than the shops. In Russia the reverse is true. When the housewife finds the shops empty, she has to go to the market. In the shops the prices are controlled by the Government; in the market by the laws of supply and demand.

The Communist theory, like so many theories, is admirable on paper, but it forgets the human factor. It is easy for statisticians to draw up plans, to determine the amount of meat, vegetables and grain needed by the industrial workers and to demand quotas from the Kolkhosi. But human beings are often stubborn and unreasonable. They dislike being dragooned and they prefer to go their own ways. What is more, a man can hardly be blamed for prefering to dispose of his goods for a high price on the open market than to watch them seized by an official for a pittance. Perhaps there will be a change of heart among the farmers as the years pass, but it will take a long time. I was given several illustrations of the difficulties. One farmer, an enthusiast, complained that another member of the group was not doing his fair share of the unpleasant jobs and he didn't see why he should get the same remuneration. A farmer's wife complained of the habits of a family which shared the same house; there were constant disagreements between them and the two men were no longer on speaking terms. Another farmer complained that one of his colleagues had hidden some of his produce to sell on the open market and was guilty of sabotage. All these disagreements are understandable and, so long as human nature remains what it is, it's difficult to see how they can be avoided.

It would be wrong to suggest that the collective farm completely eliminates private enterprise. Each member has his own two acres of land which are usually devoted to growing vegetables for his family and he will probably keep a few chickens, a pig or two and possibly a cow. In fact a constant cause of friction is the amount of time spent on the two acres for private purposes and the amount on the common land for growing food for the Government.

Collective farms often resemble a large estate in England, or even a village. There are a number of large houses and buildings, surrounded by several homesteads. But the accommodation is not always so generous. My American friend told me that at the Kolkhosi he visited, living space was severely rationed and families had to share houses, a constant cause of dispute.

The Government has a tough nut to crack as the problem is immense. It is difficult to obtain reliable statistics, but in all probability at least seventy million people are involved. Official reports give the number of households as fifteen million, which means an average of sixty-five on each Kolkhos.

The chief weapons for stimulating efficiency are the village soviets and the Communist Party. The village soviet, which is something like a parish council, is warned by the Ministry of Agriculture to keep an eye on the collective farm and the president can find himself in trouble if things go wrong. While I was in Moscow there were several plays dealing with the theme. Lazy soviets and corrupt presidents were pilloried. The urban audience applauded in the appropriate places, but I suspect their rural brothers were less enthusiastic. Farmers do not appreciate nosey-parkers, especially when they are indistinguishable from government snoopers; and my own experience as a city councillor suggests that a president of a village soviet is probably unwilling to interfere in matters about which he is not technically informed.

More formidable are the hand-picked members of the

Communist Party who live on the farms and are responsible for implementing government policy. They are a cross between missionaries and policemen! They work in groups and supervise everything. They issue posters and leaflets; expose waste and incompetence; remove officials from office and fill vacancies; regulate relations with the local soviet; produce plans and statistics; publicize successes and failures; allocate accommodation; make monetary awards. It is not surprising that in the early days some of these political busybodies were assassinated.

But it is easy to be critical. The fact is, the Government is making a gigantic effort to revolutionize agriculture so that the country can be self-supporting. The methods of the new system may be bad, but so were the results of the old. The farming community is naturally conservative and, if pressure is brought to bear upon it to make it efficient, it usually has nobody but itself to blame. Even so, it is difficult to believe that it was necessary for Stalin to have been so ruthless. The punishments were appalling and the casualties enormous.

But it would be wrong to paint too grim a picture. Much is good and stimulating in the new system. The intelligent countryman is no longer frustrated by illiteracy and lack of capital. If he wants to get on, he can, providing he is careful to walk the political tightrope. The Government encourages him to study and to make full use of scientific inventions. If he and his comrades need new equipment, the Ministry will try to provide it. And there are social amenities. My American friend was impressed by the communal buildings in the Kolkhos where plays, concerts and entertainments are provided. So often the agricultural labourer is left in a rut. He lives miles away from a town. He is denied cultural opportunities. His only recreation is the village inn. Such conditions are rapidly passing away in Russia.

More important is the change of status. In spite of the snooping, dragooning and interference, the worker on the collective farm no longer regards himself as a mere labourer, the servant of his master and the inferior to the townsman. He is a participant in a great experiment and a necessary member of the community. If he works hard and shows initiative he can get a responsible position and a good income.

Mention should be made of the State farms. They differ from the Kolkhosi in that the Ministry owns them and is directly responsible for them. Most of them are of an experimental nature. A friend visited a milk-producing unit. Special methods of breeding and feeding were employed and the quality and amount of milk were above average. He spoke enthusiastically of the cleanliness of the buildings and the efficiency of the workers.

Time alone will prove the worth of the experiment; at this juncture it is wiser to defer judgement. In England we are moving slowly toward a form of collectivization. Small farms are being bought by large companies and are merged into larger units. Economic necessity makes this tendency inevitable. Russia has moved with more haste and perhaps less speed. Stalin would have been wiser if he had been prepared to take fifty years to achieve what he tried to do in five. Argument, persuasion, experience and willing co-operation are better weapons than authoritarian compulsion and, in the end, they reap larger dividends.

My attempts to visit a Russian factory were as futile as those to see a Kolkhos. I asked repeatedly, but each day I was given a different excuse. I don't know the reason. It may have been red-tape and bureaucracy; it may have been suspicion of a Westerner; it may have been that I might have witnessed conditions not compatible with Soviet propaganda. I have read accounts of factory tours made by 'fellow-travellers' and I have not been impressed. I imagine they were granted privileges denied to me because they accepted what they were told without asking awkward questions, and never strolled from the official path. I have on my desk a booklet of a hundred pages given me by my Intourist hosts, *American Workers Look At The Soviet Union*. I was told it would answer all my questions and open my eyes. In fact it avoids the questions and opens my eyes to nothing, except the credulity of human beings who will always believe what they want to believe. Its contents can be summed up in a sentence. American industrial conditions are appalling; Soviet industrial conditions are wonderful.

Fortunately I was allowed to meet several workers and, although they doubtless told me what they were ordered to say, I was able to get an idea of factory life. This was supplemented by the information that was put at my disposal at our embassies.

When the Communists took control the country was poor, backward and undeveloped. The standard of living was deplorably low and the majority lacked the bare necessities. About that there can be no argument. In the intervening thirty-five years there have been immense strides forward. Facts may not be identical with propaganda, but we cannot forget that if it had not been for the rapid industrialization of the country, Russia would have fallen victim to Hitler. Although we may dislike many aspects of the Soviet régime, we must pay a deserved tribute to the vision of the leaders and the determination of the workers.

In Tsarist days the elementary needs of the people were not met. For instance the boot factories were sufficient to provide each man with one pair of boots once in five years. The clothing position was worse. Heavy industry was hopelessly organized. Electrical power stations were conspicuous by their absence. It was a ramshackle economy, run in the interests of private profit and it took little cognizance of the wants of society or the conditions of the workers.

Then came Lenin. He was a determined visionary. He planned to discard this outworn system and to industrialize and equip Russia so that it could be brought into line with other European countries. So began the series of Five Year Plans. Factories, power stations, railways, dams, blast-furnaces appeared in rapid succession. Old plant was modernized and coal, steel and cement supplies soared. New industries were started and, by the time of Hitler's invasion, the factories were turning out vast quantities of motor-cars, aeroplanes, tractors and rubber goods. To achieve this, the Government took over and controlled all the natural resources and means of production. Having everything in its hands, it was free to decide how the resources should be used in the interests of the people as a whole. For the first time in the history of the human race, private profit was no longer a consideration.

Such a revolutionary change in the economic basis of the national life demanded strict control and direction of labour. Factories in new districts cannot be started unless workers are moved. I was told there was no compulsion and men were free to move from job to job. I don't believe it. I said to an engineer, who showed me a photograph of a dam: 'When this dam was being built, how were the workers attracted to such a remote spot?'

'They went of their own free will.'

'Do you mean to say that married men voluntarily left their homes and lived in primitive conditions for months at a time, if they were free to apply for a job in their own city?'

'Yes.'

I can believe that the Marxist missionaries, who shared Lenin's vision, did, but I am doubtful about the rest. That, of course, is the difficulty when talking with 'reliable' workers. So far as they themselves are concerned, I am sure they speak the truth. They are ready to do as they are told and to give of their best, because they have a passionate belief in the Communist goal.

I asked the engineer about conditions in the factory where he worked. I began with an obvious question: 'Do you work hard?'

'Yes. The Soviet worker cannot be content until he has done more than he is expected to do. He must always be exceeding his standard.'

'That sounds to me dangerously like sweated labour.'

'Not in our country. We work for ourselves and everything belongs to us. There is no boss to exploit us.'

'Do you have any say in plans for production?'

'Certainly. We have many factory committees. All the workers can express their views and make suggestions. That is the only way to get improvements.'

'And are the workers interested in production?'

'Yes. Every month we have reports. And we have competitions with other factories to beat their records.'

'What social amenities are there at your factory?'

'We arrange these at our factory meetings. We have recently built a canteen and a large rest room with a stage for concerts and plays. In the summer we spend the dinner hour in the factory garden. Last year we planted trees and installed a fountain. Next year we shall have a swimming-bath.'

'I am told that at some factories there is sleeping accommodation. Is that true of your factory?'

'No. But it was when I was working in Leningrad. We had dormitories for the bachelors.'

'Do you have clubs?'

'I am not sure what you mean. But we have a Culture House, where there is a library, museum and art exhibition. And there is a nursery and kindergarten for the workers' children.'

'What are the conditions like in your workshop?'

'It used to be hot and the hygienic conditions were out of date. Now the temperature is regulated automatically and cleanliness is compulsory.'

'What about schools and continuation classes for the workers?'

'They happen all the time. All the men in my factory are

eager to go on courses. They learn about production and, when they produce more, their wages go up.'

'Have you a holiday home?'

'Yes, a beautiful one by the Black Sea. For those who work hardest, it's free. The others pay a little.'

'Do you encourage piece-work?'

'Yes. The Stakhanovite movement is an essential part of Marxist pioneering.'

'In England we don't like it. We think it leads to sweated labour.'

'That's because you work for capitalists. The harder we work, the more the country prospers.'

'But what about your comrades who are not so keen about beating targets and establishing new records?'

'Lazy workmen must be educated. When they understand the aims of Communism they will want to work.'

'May I ask you about your housing conditions?'

'Certainly.'

'Have you a flat, or a house?'

'My factory has a large apartment house. I have a big room for my wife and child and we have our own kitchen. The rent is quite small and it includes heating. Some of my meals I have in the factory canteen and I often take my wife to the films in the factory cinema. While we are there, my boy goes to the kindergarten.'

'I should love to go inside a Russian home. Would it be possible for me to call on you? And I should like to meet your wife and child.'

'I am afraid it would not be convenient.'

That question always produced the same answer. This time I threw courtesy to the winds and pressed my point.

'That's a pity. I have come to Russia to learn about your country and to understand the people. It would be such a help to meet informally. If you came to England you would receive many invitations and you would be welcome in our

Moscow University

The Moscow Soviet or City Council House

Post-war flats: a block of eight hundred in Moscow

homes. People would ask you to meals and to stay the week-end.'

'It is not our custom. And now I must ask you to excuse me.'

I wonder if Intourist realizes what a disastrous impression is made by this refusal. I am sure the Russians are as friendly and hospitable as anybody else and they must dislike treating foreigners as pariahs. My guides constantly spoke to me of the need for Anglo-Soviet friendship, but they seemed incapable of realizing that friendship results, not from political demonstrations and diplomatic pacts, but from normal human intercourse.

Toward the end of my stay in Moscow I asked Mr Rogov if he would arrange for a photographer to take a photograph of me in the Red Square.

'Why do you want a photograph?' he asked.

'As a memento of my visit.'

'Any other reason?'

'It will interest my friends in England.' And I added with a smile: 'It will prove that I have really been to Russia and walked in your streets without being locked up.'

'I will see. Perhaps it will be possible to arrange it.'

I inquired each morning, but I was told the weather was not right for a good photograph. I imagine the matter was still *sub judice* and Mr Rogov awaited the necessary permissions.

On my last day a message came to my room at breakfast to say a photographer was in the hotel lounge awaiting me. I hurried downstairs and was joined by my guide. We crossed Red Square and took up our positions near St Basil's Cathedral. The photographer took infinite pains and assured me he wanted to do a really good job. He took several photographs and seemed pleased.

'And now, what about one outside the gates of the Kremlin?' said my guide.

'That would be splendid.'

We walked forty or fifty yards and I prepared myself. The photographer was on the point of operating the camera when two men in uniform descended upon us. I do not know what was said, but there was a lengthy altercation and, as each minute passed, my guide became more embarrassed and angry. Eventually the men in uniform walked away and, as far as I could make out, exposed the film and put it in their pockets.

'What's the trouble?' I asked my guide.

'It would seem that the permission of the security officer has not been obtained.'

'But, surely, you don't have to get police permission to take a photograph in a public place?'

'Yes, of course.'

'I am glad we don't have such customs in England.'

'But I'm quite sure you do. Your Government wouldn't allow a photographer to take a photograph of me in London.'

'What nonsense! You could do as you like. Nobody would be interested. But I must say, it seems incredible that after all the coming and going for the past two days, plus the fact that I am accompanied by a government-sponsored photographer and a government-sponsored guide, we still can't have this photograph.'

'But the Kremlin is a special place. It's where the Government works.'

'My dear chap, it's no good talking like that to an Englishman. We don't care twopence about Governments.'

'But you wouldn't be allowed to take a photograph of Downing Street?'

'I don't suppose I should want to; but if I did, there's nothing to stop me.'

'And what would your Conservative Prime Minister do if he knew that you, a Socialist, stood outside his house with a camera?'

'He'd probably invite me in to take a snap of him in his bath!'

Back to the Intourist office in the hotel where nice Mr Rogov was as placid and courteous as ever. 'I shall do some telephoning,' was all he said. He was accustomed to, and perhaps enjoyed, the creakings of the bureaucratic machine. They were part of his daily diet.

The girls in the office seemed fairly free so I filled in the time by chatting with them. They asked if they might see the pectoral cross given by the Patriarch to the Archbishop of Canterbury. I fetched it from my room. They fingered it admiringly. 'Do any of you go to church?' I asked.

They laughed loudly. 'Of course not.'

'Why?'

'We've been properly educated. We know there isn't a God.'

'Do you know anything at all about Christianity?'

'Yes. It's a myth used by the capitalists to deprive the workers of their rights.'

'Do you really think my chief job in life is to pump dope into the poor?'

'No. But religion is a hangover from the past. When men hadn't the scientific knowledge to explain Nature, they took refuge in God.'

'Do you believe in spirit?'

'What do you mean?'

'Do you think there's a part of you that survives the grave?'

'No. When you're dead, you're dead.'

'And how do you think this world was made?'

'Let's leave that to the scientists. Our job is to take the world as we find it and change it.'

The argument raged furiously for half an hour, but with good humour. They were anxious not to hurt my feelings and they were never impolite. It was most interesting as the girls were products of atheistic education. They knew nothing of Christianity. Some of them had relatives who attended church. That was a pity, but, if people wished to worship, the State gave them freedom. In a few years the churches would be empty.

Mr Rogov smiled. 'All is well. The photographer awaits you. He and your guide will take you to Red Square.'

Off we went. I posed in the same positions. The officers in uniform watched in silence. As we left the gates of the Kremlin, I pointed to Lenin's tomb. 'I know it's closed, but don't you think I should be allowed to go inside to offer a prayer of thanksgiving to the Architect of Freedom?'

My guide solemnly replied: 'I'm sorry, but they have not finished embalming Stalin's body.'

Chapter Seven

HEALTH AND HAPPINESS

'*We are not only rebuilding human society on an economic basis; we are mending the human race on scientific principles.*' This slogan is posted on the Moscow Sports Club.

Because Intourist knew I was especially interested in public health, every facility was given me to inspect hospitals, clinics and experimental stations. I had long conversations with professors, doctors, nurses and superintendents and I would like to pay tribute to their patience and interest. What is more, we usually managed to escape from politics and propaganda. My hosts knew I was reasonably well informed. They were anxious to show me their achievements, but they were equally inquisitive about the health services in Britain. Although it is generally supposed that the capitalist countries reserve medicine for the rich and allow the poor to die off like flies, the men I met were too intelligent to swallow the official line. They had access to Western medical journals and they understood recent developments.

To appreciate Soviet medicine we must remember a basic doctrine of Marxism. The development of a human being is largely determined by his environment. It is the duty of the Government to create the conditions of health in order that citizens may grow up in salutary surroundings. Britain will not quarrel with the definition. The Welfare State takes full responsibility for the health of its members. Medical attention no longer depends upon purse strings and charity. Our doctors are paid handsomely by the Exchequer to look after

133

our bodies and we pride ourselves upon the fact that the well-being of the community is a national responsibility.

There is, however, a difference of emphasis between the two countries. We specialize in cures, the Soviets in causes. We spend money lavishly upon our hospital patients, the Soviets upon preventive work. Our sanatoria are an example to the rest of the world, but the Russians spend more time and money upon removing the causes of tuberculosis.

The staggering fact about Soviet medicine is not its excellence—it is unquestionably inferior to ours—but its accomplishments in thirty-five years. When the Communists came into power disease was rampant and the health services deplorable. Lenin determined to effect a revolution. He succeeded. It is true that Russia produced men of international repute—Pavlov, Speransky and Mechnikov—but nine-tenths of the population were neglected. Today conditions in rural areas are far from satisfactory, though infinitely better than they were; in the cities solid foundations have been laid and, in a generation or two, the health services will be second to none.

The basic administrative unit is the health centre. Moscow is divided into areas and the areas into districts. Each area has its clinic staffed with specialists and each district its health centre. The general practitioners work from the health centres.

When a man falls ill he gets into touch with his district health centre, and asks for the doctor of his choice. If he is confined to his bed, the doctor calls at his house. It's worth emphasizing this point because it is sometimes supposed that Soviet medicine is impersonal. An Englishman in Moscow said to me: 'I hate their system. You have to go to a huge clinic and take what's given you. I much prefer the family doctor who works from his house.' But it isn't so. The Muscovite family does have its own doctor; the only difference is, his surgery is not at his home but in the health centre. And there's a lot to be said in favour of the arrangement. The centre is well staffed with nurses and administrators. The doctor does not have to waste time on secretarial chores and minor ailments. A secretary takes down the details, and if the ailment is a minor one a competent nurse deals with it. In this way a doctor is left free to devote himself to urgent cases.

And the centres are well equipped. If a doctor wants his patient X-rayed, it can be done on the spot. He doesn't have to send him to a hospital. If he thinks a disease may be caused by faulty teeth, he can seek the advice of a dentist in a neighbouring room and, if necessary, the patient can be treated immediately.

I believe we have something to learn from the Russian system. While I am sure it's usually a good thing for a doctor to live among his people and to play his part in the locality, it's a pity he has to spend so much time doing things that could be done by less qualified people. It would be an advantage if he could establish himself at a health centre where he could avail himself of general medical service and equipment. And it would relieve pressure on the hospitals if he could be given diagnostic facilities. Hospital beds are needed for urgent surgical cases; they should not be occupied by people who could receive necessary treatment at a health centre.

I spent an afternoon at a centre in a Moscow suburb. In the hall I watched the people talking to the secretaries at the reception desk. They gave their names and the names of their doctors; the secretaries produced the appropriate files and they were directed to the surgeries. It was a pleasant combination of efficiency and friendly informality. I talked with a group of mothers. Some wanted pre-natal treatment; others to hear a lecture on home-making and diet. Women are exempted from work for six weeks before the birth of their children and they receive generous maternity grants which cover the cost of special diet and infants' clothing.

I doubt if the conditions are much different from those prevailing in England today, but they are infinitely better than those which existed in working-class areas twenty years ago. Russia certainly set the rest of the world an example of which she is justly proud and she gave motherhood a new dignity.

A clerk gave some of the women cards which entitled them to privileged places on the trams and Metro. They are able to go to reserved places without being jostled. It's the same at the shops. Providing they take their cards they can jump the queue and avoid waiting. And, if necessary, they can go to a rest home without suffering a loss of wages.

I asked a nurse what happened to the mothers in rural districts. She admitted that it was difficult to provide a proper service, but 'flying squads' of doctors are sent to Kolkhosi and larger villages and temporary advisory centres are set up.

I was struck by the crèche. While the mother was being examined she left her child in a nursery where, if it was old enough, it played games with the others. What a sensible arrangement! So often in England a consultation becomes unnecessarily difficult because the doctor has to compete with the children.

Until a child is three a mother takes it to the health centre several times a year and both are examined. In the early stages the doctor and nurse call at the house. When the child reaches school age there is a thorough overhaul and then three general inspections each year.

I watched the boys and girls being treated by the doctors and dentists. The surgery routine was the same as in this country, but the difference came when the doctor wanted an X-ray or ordered sunlight treatment; both were available in adjoining rooms.

By the time I reached the top-story it was late in the afternoon and men and women were calling at the health centre on their way from work. Several were suffering from colds, which is not surprising in view of the appalling heat in most Moscow buildings. In my hotel I invariably turned off the radiators in my bedroom and opened the windows, but as soon as I went out the radiators were immediately turned on and the windows closed! I was intrigued with the equipment for dealing with the common cold. The patient lay on a couch, and the nurse applied a pad to each nostril and turned on a machine. I did not discover what it was, but I was told it effected a cure within twenty-four hours. I asked so many questions that the nurse invited me to return for treatment if I needed it during my stay. Fortunately I didn't.

Upstairs I found the psychiatrist, though I was assured that nervous disorders were rare in Russia as everybody felt secure and contented! He, like the other doctors, had the right to order free holidays for his patients. I am sure this is a wise arrangement, and we should make more use of it. Many disorders, physical and mental, can be put right with rest and a change.

So far as the children are concerned, the holidays are planned on a large scale during the summer vacation and the doctors accompany them.

Before I left, the superintendent, a woman, took me to her office and invited me to ask questions.

'How many doctors are there at this centre?'

'Sixty-eight.'

'What is the average annual salary?'

'The junior doctors get £300 and the seniors £1000.'

'Does the doctor spend all his time at the centre?'

'No. He's here for consultations, but he does his rounds in the usual way. Most of them have their own districts.'

'Does this mean that all the people living in a district must have a particular doctor?'

'No. There may be three or four doctors in a district and the people can choose. If they don't like any of them, they can apply for somebody else.'

'For how long do the doctors train?'

'They attend a medical institute for six years.'

'You seem to have a large staff of nurses. What is the proportion?'

'Two nurses to a doctor.'

'Will you tell me something about training and pay?'

'A nurse begins training at seventeen. The course lasts two years. She then does special work for a year according to her bent and she finishes with one year's practical work. Salaries vary according to experience, but most of them get between £150 and £250.'

The health centre was filling up, and I could see that the staff had enough on their hands without talking to me, so, after a brief visit to the dentists' surgery where I watched an extraction, I withdrew.

A day or two later I was taken to the hospital belonging to the Ministry of Transport. It was an impressive building, twenty years old. It had an attractive approach and a grandiose reception hall. I was met by the Medical Officer who wore a smart green tunic with plenty of gold braid. I quickly gained the impression that he was immensely proud of this hospital and was keen to show me everything. I was told by my guide that his enthusiasm and hard work were largely responsible for its success. He took me to the cloakroom where I was given the usual white coat and then we went to his magnificent office. On the walls were portraits of pioneers in Russian medicine. After we had sat around his desk he phoned the senior consultant and I was invited to bombard them with questions.

'Why does this hospital belong to the Ministry of Transport?'

'Each district has its own general hospital, but there are additional hospitals for particular diseases and particular groups of people. In this instance we cater for workers who are on the move. If a man is engaged in transport it may be difficult for him to attend his local hospital, so he can come to one of the eleven Traffic Hospitals in Moscow.'

'How many beds are there?'

'Seven hundred and twenty.'

'Is the hospital reserved for men?'

'No. We take both sexes.'

'What are the main departments?'

'Surgery, Gynaecology, Therapy, Tuberculosis, and Ear, Nose and Throat.'

'Tell me about tuberculosis. Does your treatment differ from ours?'

'I shouldn't think so, except that possibly we are devoting a great deal of time, thought and money to preventive work. B.C.G. is compulsory and the results are most encouraging. If patients are well enough to work we provide them with night sanatoria; this reduces the chances of infection. And there are separate canteens in the factories.'

'Are you making use of special drugs?'

'At the moment we are experimenting with *pask* and *vtevasite*; both are used with antibiotics.'

'What are your views about smoking? Do you think it affects the lungs adversely?'

'I think my colleague had better answer that one.' And here the consultant chipped in: 'That's a moot point. It would be unwise to express a definite opinion. But there are medical men in the Soviet Union, perhaps an increasing number, who think the non-smokers have a better chance of escaping infection. What is the view in England?'

'Probably the same. My own Medical Officer of Health in Bristol refuses to commit himself, but I notice that he has given up smoking!'

Next we turned to staffing and salaries.

'What is your hospital establishment?'

'A hundred and fourteen, three-quarters of whom are women.'

'That seems an unusually high proportion.'

'Not in the Soviet Union. There are more women than men in the medical profession.'

'What are the rates of pay?'

'A nurse gets £150–200 p.a.; a junior doctor £300–360 a consultant, £1,000–2,000. But you must remember that in addition to the salary, there are concessions for holidays meals and accommodation. The actual salary is only part of the total remuneration.'

We passed to general health problems.

'Are you concerned with preventive work, apart from what you have already told me about tuberculosis?'

'At this hospital we naturally give most of our time to helping people who are already ill, but the emphasis in the Soviet Union is upon removing the causes of disease. Plenty of food, good wages, satisfactory housing, adequate pensions sick benefits, maternity grants, holiday homes are the best weapons with which to fight sickness. I think that England is giving more attention to these things now?'

'Yes. We have our insurance and health schemes and we have built thousands of houses since the war for renting cheaply to the working classes.'

'And what about the man without money who wants to become a doctor?'

'There is nothing to prevent him, providing he has the brains. His training at university and hospital can be paid for by the State.'

My guide suggested at this point that I might like to make a tour of the hospital. The doctor rose from his chair and said, 'Now, Canon Stockwood, it's up to you to say where you want to go. You are free to wander where you will and to talk to anybody.'

I took him at his word. I wandered along corridors and stopped whenever a ward took my interest. They were clean and well equipped. The beds were smaller than ours and placed more closely together. And the wards were not so big, but more homely. I talked freely with the patients, who were as eager to demonstrate their aches and pains as are my parishioners.

There were six operating theatres, all of which were up to our standards, and the Medical Officer showed me with pride the most recent collection of surgical instruments. Every precaution was taken against infection and I was politely requested not to touch the tables.

I was surprised at the amount of space given to steam and mud baths as I thought they were no longer in vogue, but I was told that transport workers were prone to rheumatism and found the baths a help. The Medical Officer tried to prove his point by taking me to the cellars where the different sorts of mud were stored in large tanks and expounding the virtues of each of them.

I enjoyed my visit to this hospital and the Medical Officer impressed me as much as anybody I met in Russia. He probably makes the right political noises and does everything a good Soviet citizen should do, but he is wedded to his job and would be a credit to any community. Especially did I like his wide grasp of health problems. If he is ever allowed to visit England, he will be a welcome guest.

The Soviet view of life insists that health cannot be divorced from culture. If human beings are to achieve wholeness, they must live in the right environment. That is why importance is attached to surroundings and leisure.

The Metro is world-famous and photographs of a new station often appear in Western papers, but its astonishing grandeur only becomes fully apparent when one sees it for oneself. There are thirty-nine stations, most of which are the size of a cathedral. Each is beautifully decorated and each is different. In some are sculptures and busts; in others mosaics and paintings. I have a vivid recollection of the station dedicated to the great military figures in Russian history. There were eight mosaics, one of which is composed of more than two million pieces of stone. It is an astonishing accomplishment. I remember with less pleasure another mosaic of a mother and child, the symbols of the Russian people, looking with adoring eyes at a deified Stalin. Underneath in letters of gold are the words: 'Peace throughout the world.' It was a distasteful parody of the Virgin and Child and the Christmas message.

The air is changed seven times an hour and there is neither smell nor stuffiness. The contrast with the London tubes was remarkable.

What I appreciated most was the quiet. The trains, which drew in at either side of the vast hall, seemed to move noiselessly and were hardly noticeable. The passengers were dwarfed by the buildings and obtruded themselves as little as a congregation in St Paul's Cathedral. Bad behaviour and smoking are not tolerated and everything is done to create an atmosphere of reverent spaciousness. I often travel in the London Underground and invariably feel tired and unnerved as a result; my experience on the Moscow Metro stimulated a feeling of restfulness. I am certain that the unconscious impression made upon the millions of Muscovites who use this system of transport each day must be good and uplifting.

I have already referred to the reservations on the Metro for pregnant mothers. This prompted me to ask my guide whether there were privileges for other groups.

'No, but elderly people always receive special consideration.'

'And what about the railways?'

'The same applies. But, of course, there are different classes.'

'How many?'

'Three, and sometimes four: deluxe, tourist, ordinary and standing.'

'That does not fit in with my idea of an egalitarian society. In England we have only two classes.'

'Capitalist, and non-capitalist?'

'No. The only people who can afford to travel first class are the bureaucrats whose tickets are paid for by the taxpayer.'

In their drive for culture and a cheerful environment, the Government is beginning to realize the importance of clothes —and not before it is time. They appreciate, at last, that drabness is not a corollary of a healthy society though, to be fair, during the early days of the Revolution money and resources had to be diverted to essential capital expenditure.

The masters of fashion rule from a five-story building near the centre of the city called the Central House of Fashion Design. I was invited to a mannequin parade. I am bound to admit I was alarmed because, when it comes to women's clothes, I am out of my depth. However, I went and the experience was rewarding.

On the ground floor was a big showroom with another hall for the display. Both rooms were filled with women and I was the only male. I was interested in those who had come to see. A few were expensively dressed in fur coats and long skirts, but most were in working clothes with scarves over their heads. The children were much more attractive; they wore bright blouses and pretty pinafores.

Demonstrators explained the dresses to the crowd who, in spite of the notice 'Do not touch', fingered the material, asked many questions and discussed the models. These costumes were for exhibition only, but the replicas could be bought in dozens of shops in Moscow and all the main cities. An official told me that, in recent years, great efforts had been made to manufacture colourful materials inspired by regional traditional costumes. She showed me a variety of cotton dresses with attractive machine-made embroideries.

I asked about prices. She quoted these examples: coat and skirt for office wear, £30; autumn coat, £12 10s.; summer slacks, £2 10s.; cotton print frock, £3; afternoon dress trimmed with machine embroidery, £7 10s.; long black velvet dress, £12 10s.; indoor frock of red material for winter, £10; crêpe de Chine dance frock, £15.

I inquired whether customers had the dresses made for them in the shops or 'fashion studios' as she called them. She replied that most bought the patterns and the material, reducing the cost by twenty per cent.

Three of the four mannequins in the parade were youngish and pretty, but homely rather than elegant; the fourth was middle-aged and rather stout. The demonstrator announced the number of the gown, and the mannequin walked twice around the dais for little more than a minute. The spectators made notes and asked questions. Special attention was paid to outsize models and to dresses for pregnant women and the reaction of the spectators was closely watched by representatives of the designers and producers. At one point the demonstrator remarked: 'There is no reason why stout women should not be well dressed. Look at this model.'

The dresses tended to lack elegance but were well cut. The evening gowns had full skirts and high necklines. Emphasis is on the word 'modesty'; sex appeal does not play a big part in Soviet fashions.

Toward the end of the afternoon it was the turn of the men, though there was only one model. The suits, two-piece, were well below British standards and expensive. A heavy brown jacket and trousers cost £40, and a blue suit in light cotton material for summer wear £20. The demonstrator singled out the felt hat, priced at £2, for general interest because Muscovites are being encouraged to exchange their ugly cloth caps for trilbies. Attention was also paid to the model's shoes, serviceable but poorly finished. They cost £8. I told my guide I thought the prices were a bit excessive; he

eplied that the clothes I had seen were above average and
here were cheaper lines.

When the display was over, I went to the stocking and hat
departments and watched the women finger nylons at £1 a
pair. Then I was taken to the manager's office and plied with
questions about British fashions. Norman Hartnell's fame
has now penetrated the Iron Curtain, though it is thought that
he and his fellow designers are interested only in court circles
and are content for the working classes to make what use they
can of cast-off mis-shapen clouts. But Hartnell is given full
marks for resisting Dior, whose skirt lengths are not appreciated, perhaps because they hardly fit a somewhat puritanical
régime, besides being inappropriate for the Russian winds.

In spite of the misconceptions, I was encouraged by the fact
that there was an interest in Western designs and standards.
Until Stalin's death it was heresy, or worse, to suggest that
Britain and France might be examples in the world of dress
design.

The manager, who became increasingly friendly during our
conversation, gave me an attractive fashion magazine. I was
surprised at this, because I knew the authorities were reluctant
to allow such magazines to leave the country. And not without
reason. Shortly after the war, when Russia was licking her
wounds and mourning her dead, an American journalist
obtained some fashion plates and lampooned them in New
York. In a smart store there was a double mannequin parade
—the first showed how the American women dressed, the
second the Russian. The contrast produced roars of laughter.
It was one of those occasions which show how a certain type
of American is a past-master in bad taste and vulgarity. As
I turned over the pages of the magazine I asked the manager
whether it had a wide circulation. He told me it was read
by the fashion designers and producers thoughout the country.

'But what about the ordinary people? What are you doing
to interest them?'

'We do a certain amount through magazines and news-papers, but we depend chiefly upon displays.'

'But when do the workers find time to come to the displays?'

'They don't, but we go to them. In most of the large factories we have parades and in the summer we have demonstrations in the parks. These are very popular and hundreds come.'

'Do you feel you are making progress?'

'Certainly; but you must remember that for generations most of our people were too poor to dress properly. It was no good them taking an interest in clothes, because they knew they could never afford them. Today it is different. People have the money with which to furnish their wardrobes simply. They are keen to learn, but it's bound to take time before we reach a really good standard. We shan't be satisfied until we make our Communist country the best-dressed country in the world.'

That fits into the general picture. Health demands beautiful surroundings, a beautiful underground and beautiful clothes. Without these conditions the Soviet man is incomplete.

The Government's educational drive is in full force in the large Maxim Gorky Culture Park, on the banks of the river Moskva. Until just before the war it was waste land, a dumping ground for junk. Now it is the headquarters of Soviet recreation and it is patronized by thousands.

It costs sixpence to enter and near the admission barriers are large posters with details of the day's entertainments. Concerts, dances, art exhibitions, ballet, chess tournaments, films, lectures, fashion parades, children's competitions are included in the programme. In some ways it is like Hyde Park, but there is more organized activity.

The theatre is surrounded by trees and can seat a big audience. It reminded me of the open-air opera house in

Rome. The incredible artist Ulanova, perhaps the greatest ballerina in the world, attracts thousands. When she performs at the Bolshoi the queues are enormous, but in the Culture Park she delights a much bigger audience.

Not far away is the 'Fun Fair' with the usual attractions. Englishmen who enjoy a holiday at Blackpool would be equally happy here. And, of course, there are trips on the river, either in miniature steamers or rowing boats. The sound of a gramophone from a passing canoe brings nostalgic memories of a picnic on the Granta near Byron's Pool on a lovely June day when the tripos was over.

The Library is in a quiet spot and to it go the more serious minded. There is a good assortment of books and periodicals—all of them in strict conformity with the party line. Some are reading, others making notes and a few students are obviously catching up with their essays.

The art exhibition is interesting. Picture after picture shows the glories of Soviet history. I am not an authority on painting, but I know sufficient to realize that the standard is poor. The artists seem more anxious to prove their political reliability than to grapple with the problems of colour and form. But that is not surprising because, under Stalin, Soviet art has reached its nadir. However, judging by the exclamations of the onlookers, the critics are easily pleased. A monstrously bad portrait of Stalin visiting the Red armies is enthusiastically applauded. I've visited many galleries in my time, but I don't think I've seen a worse or more incompetent painting. In England the executor would not find employment even as a pavement artist.

How different is the Chess Pavilion. In Russia everybody seems to play chess and children talk about it as much as our own youngsters discuss football. People of all ages, from seven to seventy, are sitting at the tables and a coach is giving useful advice. The spectators are outspoken: 'That's a stupid move'; 'You ought to have done this'; 'Well done. You've got him now'; 'You'll never make a chess player'; 'Come on, dad, if you aren't careful the boy will have you whacked'; 'Bravo, grandma! You're a cunning old woman. They'll be giving you a Stalin prize if you go on like this'.

A young couple finish their game and I follow them to the dancing square. On their way they stop at some athletic contests and trials of strength. The girl is not interested and she becomes impatient. In a few minutes they are waltzing. Everything is very proper. As the dancers whirl around they keep their distance; in the intervals there is no 'spooning'—in fact the sort of scenes which we take for granted in English parks are prohibited in the Culture Park.

The Children's City is quite splendid. Parents leave their children with attendants who keep an eye on them while they pass from one amusement to another—swings, toys, merry-go-rounds, miniature houses, parachute jumps, model railways, flying chairs. Lenin and Stalin look down in amazement and there are the usual Marxist slogans, but the youngsters don't seem unduly perturbed. And, of course, there are models of tractors, plans of collective farms, statistics and all the paraphernalia of Soviet propaganda, but they do little trade in such a jolly Fun Fair.

Although communal enjoyment seems to be the fashion quite a few lounged in the Culture Park by themselves with a book or chatted in small groups.

As always, vodka was in evidence. And there are more drunks in the Maxim Gorky Culture Park in a day than in Hyde Park in a year. I don't believe in prohibition, but it wouldn't do the population of Moscow any harm to 'go dry' for a year.

I don't quite know what to say about the art galleries I visited because the criteria by which one judges paintings in the Soviet Union are quite different from ours. We are interested in colour, form, contours, subjects and expression, but not the Russians. I argued these points with my guide, but he told me my approach was *bourgeois*. For him the key to artistic understanding is to be found in the article on painting in the *Great Soviet Encyclopedia* to which my attention was directed. Here is the relevant passage: 'Thanks to the efforts of the Bolshevist Party, the process of the corruption of art was arrested. The development of painting became an affair for the State, and was the object of the Party's and Government's concern. From the beginning the Party directed the painters toward an art full of ideas, of content, of truth, an art close to the people. The Party strove against the anti-Communist and anti-national tendencies that had manifested themselves in the attempts to ignore the ties that bound the young Soviet painter to the revolutionary reality and the popular masses. The principle of realistic socialism formulated by Stalin laid down the laws of the evolution of Soviet painting.'

I saw several exhibitions and I wandered around numerous galleries and museums. I was not impressed. Picture after picture depicted incidents in Stalin's life. It was propaganda at its most boring. Occasionally there was evidence of originality, but usually the painter had made political correctness the be-all and end-all of his effort. Now and again I noticed a blank space on the wall from which a painting had been removed, and sometimes a picture was covered. I suspect that in both cases the subjects had fallen into disfavour. Perhaps some of them had illustrated incidents in the life of Beria who had recently been denounced as a saboteur. Most countries have to tolerate one poet-laureate, but it's a little much when all artists become creatures of the Government. When my guide took me to the gallery which glorified the uprising in 1917, I asked him to lead me to a painting of Trotsky, without whom the Revolution might have failed. It was a leg-pull which was not appreciated! He, like most of Stalin's earlier associates, had been relegated to the rubbish heap.

The sad thing is, the galleries are besieged by hundreds and hundreds of sightseers. I have seen nothing like it in England. In our municipal galleries one encounters small groups, but in Moscow the people come in crowds. On Saturday afternoon I was one of five thousand in a gallery and there were queues waiting outside. Why they come I cannot imagine, because there is little to edify—only miles and miles of canvases to uphold the party line.

Fortunately there were signs of a slight improvement. Rooms that had been closed for several years were being re-opened and all of them contained pre-Revolutionary paintings. Nobody knows the treasures that may be tucked away in the cellars of Moscow; if they are as good as the few I saw Russia will once again become a port of call for the art traveller.

The emphasis on culture is apparent in the number and quality of the libraries. Most of them were good and well patronized. I spent several hours in the large Lenin Library. In 1917 it housed one million books; today sixteen million. It is open from nine o'clock in the morning to midnight and five thousand people pass through its turnstiles each day. The reading rooms were packed, and students were busily making notes at the writing tables. I asked to be shown the collection of English works, which were chiefly by Shakespeare and Dickens, but there was a beautiful Bible which had belonged to Westminster Abbey in the thirteenth century.

When I came to the department for periodicals, I noticed the *Daily Worker*.

'Is that the only British paper the people can read?' I asked.

'No,' replied my guide. 'We have *The Times* and the *Manchester Guardian*.'

'Where are they?'

'In another room.'

'Can I go there?'

'No, a special permit is required.'

'Does everybody wanting to read them require a permit?'

'Yes.'

'So that means that, except for the privileged few, life in England is judged by the parodies in the *Daily Worker*.'

'Why do you refer to it as a parody? Isn't the Dean of Canterbury one of the directors?'

'I believe he is, but that makes it no less of a parody.'

The Russian people love the theatre and each night during my stay in Moscow I noticed the queues. I went several times and was impressed by the standard of acting. In nearly every case the theme was political. I did not like it, but at least it was a change from sex. We found ourselves in collective farms, factories, village soviets and sanatoria. Invariably somebody had been a deviationist or a saboteur and a member of the Party detected the crime. The offender acknowledged his guilt, expressed contrition for his *bourgeois* and reactionary tendencies and promised to do better in the future. The final scene sang the praises of the Soviet era. I was reminded of my visit to Caux when I saw on the stage the possibilities of a new society when everybody had been indoctrinated with Moral Rearmament.

I am not suggesting that the Russian theatre is bad, but simply that one gets a little tired of wallowing in political propaganda. My guide, of course, disagreed with me. 'This is not propaganda,' he said. 'We show on the stage the true facts of Soviet life, and we depict Soviet man as he is. By so doing the people who see the play are encouraged to play their part in the reconstruction of our country. And that is much better than what happens in England. Most of your plays are obscene, and degrade the good things in life. Your theatre is the opposite to ours, it is an escape from reality.' Perhaps my guide was partly right. Even so there are some forms of escape that are not wholly bad. I still don't see why I shouldn't enjoy a musical comedy, or a pantomime, or a play which deals with the unimportant but amusing sides of daily life.

My visit to the Kremlin showed me another side of Soviet culture, a desire to preserve historical continuity, providing it is made clear that pre-Revolution history is important for two reasons only: (*a*) to expose the wickedness of the Tsarist régime; (*b*) to applaud the heralds of the Marxist dawn.

I never thought I should be allowed inside the Kremlin and therefore never asked. But one day nice Mr Rogov, the head of the Intourist department at my hotel, told me he wanted four photographs of myself as I was to be privileged to enter the holy of holies. It was an unforgettable experience.

The Kremlin is a fortress on a hill in the middle of the city. It is flanked by buildings, offices and cathedrals and is surrounded by massive walls. It used to be a home of the Tsars: it is now the headquarters of the Soviet régime.

My guide took me and two others to the drawbridge, where I was examined by the sentries. They handed us over to an M.V.D. officer, who never left us. My passport, which had been taken from me at the airport, was returned for the occasion and was inspected at different points during the tour: so also were my photographs.

The cathedrals, built in the fifteenth century, were magnificent. Some had recently been restored, others were in the process. Although everything seemed ready for use, they are kept as show-pieces; worship in them is prohibited. I stood in front of the high altar and said to myself the consecration prayer from the Anglican communion service in the hope and expectation that one day the Lord's table will be restored to its proper purpose. But credit must be given to the Soviet authorities for the care and attention that have been lavished upon their buildings. Everything was in its correct place, beautifully painted and polished. The vestments, dozens of them, were preserved in glass cases and at any moment one imagined the priests would arrive to sing High Mass.

The guide took us to the private apartments of the Tsars.

Again, every effort had been made to keep them exactly as they had been before the Revolution. The guide's account of the behaviour of the Tsars was interesting. We were, of course, told about their wealth, cruelty and indifference, but there was, nevertheless, pride in their accomplishments. Nationalism seemed stronger than Marxist propaganda. An Englishman in the party, when shown the royal relics, asked to be taken to the tomb of the last Tsar! The request caused some embarrassment.

Next came the Hall of the Knights of St George. It was strangely impressive. On the walls in letters of gold were the names of the great military leaders, most of whom had been officers in the Tsar's army. All the great victories in Russian history had been celebrated here. And it was here, my guide told me, Stalin had toasted the Russian people after the defeat of Hitler. He repeated the words: 'I drink first of all to the health of the Russian people because they are the most outstanding nation among all the nations that belong to the Soviet Union. I drink my toast to the health of the Russian people because it has deserved, during the war, to be recognized by all as the directing force of the Soviet Union, among all the people of our country. I drink this toast to the health of the Russian people, not only because it is a ruling people, but also because it possesses a clear mind, a tenacious character, and patience.' Strange words! The international revolutionary had succumbed to national sentiment. One day the Communists, as a whole, may learn from Stalin's temporary lapse. Patriotism is ingrained in most of us—and it is not necessarily jingoism. We can love our country, be proud of her and want to serve her, without looking down upon others or excusing our past mistakes. And any culture worth preserving must be rooted in historical tradition. The Hall of the Knights of St George will survive long after the stupid canvases in the Lenin gallery have been consigned to the flames.

The tour finished in the Hall of the Supreme Soviet. Here

the parliament of the Soviet Union meets from time to time to hear the speeches of the mighty. Everything was *de luxe*—the lighting, the walls, the chairs, the diplomatic gallery, the reception lobby. My American friend mounted the dais where Stalin had delivered his orations and treated us to a cheerful, but scurrilous, homily. The police stepped forward and made a careful inspection. They seemed deeply disturbed. Perhaps he had concealed a bomb which would send the Kremlin rocketing. The prank may not have been in the best of taste, but it was difficult to hide a smile. And one day, when Soviet culture is less *de nouveau*, the Russians will be able to share the joke.

Chapter Eight

GOING TO VOTE

ONE can learn a lot about a country from its electoral system. I have been an active participant in England and a delighted spectator in Ireland. I remember the people turning out in their thousands to cheer Mr Churchill in 1945 and immediately voting against him. A Communist acquaintance in another country, who admired the Prime Minister, was surprised by the result and sorry. 'I liked your Mr Churchill. It's a pity we shan't see him again.'

'Why shan't we see him again?' I asked.

'Well, Labour has won and they'll get rid of him.'

I tried my best to explain that however much Englishmen may disagree about programmes, they rarely allow their politics to interfere with their friendships. He was at a loss to understand. It was clear to him that a political opponent must be liquidated.

As for Dublin, I have never enjoyed an election so much. There seemed to be as many parties as candidates and I had no idea what they were all about. But a great time was had by all. Laughter, fights, cat-calls took possession of the halls, but everybody went home in the highest spirits, many dropping into the public houses on the way to liquidate their differences.

Unfortunately there was no election in Russia during my stay in Moscow, but I did my best to discover what happened. It wasn't easy because our systems have little in common. We believe that the electorate has the right to choose between different ways of running the country. The Russians deny this. They maintain there is only one way and the most the electorate can do is to select suitable people to control the pre-ordained programme.

Each town has its own soviet, which is elected by ballot in alternate years. These soviets are like our county councils. They control hospitals, schools, housing, roads, forestry; and they take care of poor families and old people. Then there are soviets for each republic. It is not always realized in England that what we call Russia is really an association of republics which are supposed to be autonomous. I suspect they have as much autonomy as Wales and Scotland have in our constitution.

The supreme body of the Union of Socialist Soviet Republics is divided into two. One chamber consists of representatives of the different republics. Sixty nationalities control about six hundred members. The second is called the Soviet of the Union. The six hundred deputies are elected for a four-year term of office; each deputy, who is chosen by ballot, represents a region with about three hundred thousand electors. The two chambers, which meet rarely, appoint a Council of People's Commissars which is the equivalent of our Cabinet. The Chairman of the Council is, to all intents and purposes, the Prime Minister.

For several years after the Revolution, voting to these bodies was by show of hands and only productive workers could take part. But since the new constitution in 1936 there has been universal suffrage and there is supposed to be a secret ballot.

The voter is presented with a list of candidates and is invited to write 'Yes' or 'No' against the names. Not all the candidates are members of the Communist Party; in fact the majority are not. This does not mean they are opposed to the policies of the Party. Quite the contrary, because all have been previously screened and pronounced politically reliable.

This is a point worth emphasizing because it gives rise to misunderstanding in England. The Communist Party is a small body. It probably consists of less than ten per cent of the nation. It is, however, the *only* political body in the Soviet

Union and it can be likened to a missionary church. It is careful about its membership and people cannot easily join. All sorts of examinations and reports are necessary before a man can become one of the *élite*. Obviously the business of government cannot depend upon this chosen handful. There are just not enough Communists to fill the positions. So people who, although they are not actually members of the Party, are in active sympathy with it are called in. But the lot of these non-party politicians is not a bed of roses. They are subjected to constant scrutiny and electors are encouraged to publicize their shortcomings. The factories, the collective farms, the newspapers are invited to voice their complaints.

To us democracy means choosing somebody to represent us. Once we have done that we usually leave him to do his job. If we don't like him we throw him out next time. To the Russians democracy means gingering up the entire community to execute a Marxist programme. The country is studded with committees—insurance committees, factory committees, farm committees, industrial committees. These committees are not debating societies; in fact they would be very foolish to discuss policy; but they are encouraged to criticize ways and means of fulfilling programmes and to expose incompetence and corruption.

To understand Russian democracy we must come to grips with the basic doctrines of Marxism. It's easy for us to dismiss their particular brand of democracy as bogus, but we must remember that we approach it from an entirely different angle. It is equally difficult for a man who has been indoctrinated with Marxism to appreciate our system. He believes we have no real freedom, and that our affairs are controlled, not by the people's representatives in Parliament, but by the pursestrings of the capitalists.

1. The Marxist asserts that the pattern of society is determined, not by ideas, but by economic facts. If a particular group is in control of a country's resources, society will

be run in a particular way, irrespective of what men may think. For instance, he looks at England and says—as indeed my guide did—'You have your Conservative, Liberal and Labour parties, but it doesn't matter what any of them say at election times, the result is always the same. The ruling class holds the reins and they will never let the reins slip from their hands.'

Put simply, we say that action is determined by thought. We run our country in a particular way, because we think it's the right one. The Marxist denies this. He says that everything depends upon the ownership of the means of production. It doesn't matter what anybody thinks because, in fact, action is determined by economics. He would try to prove his thesis by pointing to our educational and legal systems and to our religion. Our laws, according to him, help the rich to retain their property and their privileges; they penalize the dispossessed. A rich man can make thousands on the stock exchange and help himself from his neighbour's pocket by price mechanisms and no action is taken against him. A poor man can take a few shillings from a till and he will find himself in gaol.

Our schools are, according to the Marxist, calculated to give the ruling classes a superior education. There are the private schools that only the rich can afford. For the majority there is an elementary education—good enough to make them profitable to their employers, but not sufficiently good to become a threat.

Similarly, our religion. 'God bless the squire and his relations, and keep us in our proper stations.' My guide was insistent upon this—'Your Church tells the people to turn the cheek to the rich man, to put up with their sufferings and everything will come right in the next world. That's why we hate religion. We say we must put things right in this world. But you cannot alter religion. It always has been the tool of the possessing classes.'

Economic determinism, like most theories, contains some truth and is useful as a partial explanation of aspects of our society. But it fails hopelessly when it seeks to explain everything. This is especially true when it is applied to political systems. In recent years the economic basis of British society has been radically altered by Acts of Parliament and only a purblind doctrinaire would attempt to deny this. But a Marxist does. Parliament is an appendage of the capitalist system. Its legislation is determined by the wealthy and always operates in their favour. I admit the influences of economics upon our thinking and, no doubt, there are Members of Parliament who think certain things because they have been born in certain circumstances; had they grown up in a different set of circumstances their outlook, culture and standards would probably have been different. But that is not the whole story. British politics have been profoundly affected by men who have thought in wide and generous terms and have often worked against their own monetary interests for the sake of the community.

2. Related to economic determinism is the doctrine of dialectical materialism. The Marxist believes that history is the product of the struggle, often an unconscious one, between the owning and non-owning classes. Theorists, poets and preachers may draw their blue prints, but in fact the lines of development are laid down by the outcome of the class struggle. It is not that one of the rival armies is victorious over the other and changes places, but that the conflict is temporarily resolved by a jump into another pattern of society. For instance, in the Middle Ages the owning class consisted of the feudal lords, the non-owning class of tenants, villeins and serfs. The tension between the two was overcome because, for a variety of reasons, the dispossessed drifted toward the towns and became the precursors of capitalism. But as soon as they had obtained their freedom they became the masters of the new society and found themselves in

conflict with the less fortunate who, because they owned no capital or lacked skill and brain, were dependent upon them.

And what happens next? This is what Karl Marx says—and however annoyingly inadequate we find it, it's worth bearing in mind, because the Russians, who quoted it to me on several occasions, look upon it as an infallible pronouncement: 'The modern *bourgeois* society that has sprouted from the ruins of feudal society has not done away with class antagonisms. It has but established new classes, new conditions of oppression, new forms of struggle in place of the old ones. Our epoch, the epoch of the *bourgeoisie*, possesses, however, this distinctive feature: it has simplified the class antagonisms. Society as a whole is more and more splitting into two great hostile camps, into two great classes directly facing each other—*bourgeoisie* and proletariat.'

If one accepts this analysis, it's easy to understand why Communists repudiate the allegation that they are inciting class warfare: they insist that the struggle between the classes, which is basically a struggle over the ownership of the means of production, is a fact whether we are aware of it or not. At times it may show itself, e.g. when there are strikes, shortages of labour, famines, but it's always there and, like an octopus, entwines itself around everything.

Real democracy, according to them, begins when the tension between *bourgeoisie* and proletariat is resolved by the abolition of capitalism and the substitution of socialism. There can be no true 'rule by the people' so long as the capital resources of a nation and the means of production are owned and controlled by private groups. Consequently parliamentary democracy is an illusion. It is a façade to hide the deep economic inequalities that make true democracy impossible.

But the Communists are not usually concerned to gain control of Western parliamentary institutions. They prefer to achieve their ends by easier methods. To obtain a majority means convincing a large section of the electorate. And that,

say the least, is an improbability. Much better to create
ups or soviets in industry, the fighting services, the trade
ions, the public services and, by wrecking tactics, bring
wn the country in economic ruins. In their defence it must
added that they believe they are hastening an inevitable
ocess. They do not, they assert, cause the collapse; it is
ought about by the contradictions within the capitalist
stem. Their function is to shake the tree on which the fruit
already ripe.

All this may seem to us a little tiresome and stupid, but
e must understand the Marxist viewpoint if we are to
preciate their different valuations of Western and Eastern
ected assemblies. The fact that Communist candidates
casionally stand for parliament should not mislead us. The
ommunist Party does not expect the candidate to be success-
l, but the campaign provides a propaganda platform. No
oubt tributes are paid to our parliamentary institutions, but
ey mean nothing. The candidate, like every other Com-
unist, believes that the Marxist Utopia will come, not as a
sult of parliamentary legislation, but by the overthrow of
apitalism in the dialectical struggle. And this struggle is
ooted in the economic rhythm of society.

Once the new order has been established there is, according
the Marxist, an entirely new situation. Because the capital
sources and the means of production have been nationalized,
ension between the classes has been abolished. No longer are
ere 'owners' and 'non-owners'. Everything belongs to
verybody, and instead of contending armies there is a con-
ented community. Hence the business of government fulfils
new function. Instead of being a repressive weapon to keep
power the owning class, it has become the instrument for
urthering the general welfare. Again, it is no use being
ritated. The Marxist has made himself believe this. That
s why in Russia there are no opposition parties. I tried to
rgue the point with some trade unionists in Moscow when

we were discussing freedom. They had asked me why the British and American Governments were unwilling to agree the Soviet suggestions for the unification of Germany.

'There are many reasons,' I replied, 'but one of the ch is the Communist attitude toward free elections.'

'That should be no difficulty because we believe in fr elections. In fact the Stalin constitution insists upon them

'Unfortunately, words can convey different meanings different people. To a Westerner a free election implies t possibility of any political party to put forward its candidat and for the electorate to vote by secret ballot. In my ow country it means that when we have in power a Labou Government that has nationalized transport and steel, a Con servative Opposition can go to the hustings with the delibera policy of undoing the socialist economy and restoring tran port and steel to private enterprise. What is more, th Labour Party, if it happens to be in power at the time of th election, has the solemn duty of providing the Conservativ Opposition with the necessary facilities and protections t state their case in the hope of convincing the electorate.'

'But that's madness!'

'From your point of view it may be, but it's part and parce of freedom.'

'But you cannot have great economic upsets with every change of government and the restoration of class warfare.'

'I know it's inconvenient, but it's the price that has to b paid for liberty. And in any case the economic system wi not always be changing. Sooner or later the country will mak up its mind. If nationalization is more efficient than privat enterprise and produces more and better goods, the electorat will eventually insist upon it. But in your country the las word does not rest with the people; a particular economi system is forced upon them and they have to put up with whether they want it or not—and God help them if they pu forward an alternative.'

'You are wrong. Our people are free to vote as they please.'

'I agree they are free to choose from the candidates on the official list. But that's not freedom. In England it would mean that the Prime Minister would give each constituency a list with twenty names, each belonging to his own party, and tell the electorate to choose ten.'

'But not everybody on the list in Soviet elections is a member of the Communist Party.'

'I know, but the so-called non-party candidates dare not set themselves up as an opposition on the understanding that, if returned to power, they would modify or abolish the Marxist economy.'

'But nobody in the Soviet Union would wish to do that, therefore your point about an opposition does not arise. There are no classes in our country, so there can be no rival parties. We are a socialist society so there is only need for one party. And that is what the people want.'

'If you are so certain the people want it, why don't you have free elections as we in the West understand them? After all, you have nothing to fear because, if your estimate is correct, the opposition candidates would forfeit even more deposits than do the Liberals in England! But I realize that in the present set-up nobody would dare to come forward. But in Germany it's different. There the situation is comparatively fluid. In the Eastern zone the people have had a chance to appreciate the benefits of a Communist régime. If these benefits are as magnificent as we are led to suppose, the people will be clamouring for larger and larger doses of Marxism. So you have nothing to fear. You are bound to win hands down.'

'The people in East Germany are free to vote as they choose.'

'That is sheer nonsense. At the last election one either voted publicly or at a ballot box after one's name had been

taken. I've been to Germany myself and talked to leading me
of the utmost integrity and they all say the same thing. Th
Communist handling of elections, like the Nazis before, is
parody of justice.'

It was, of course, useless to argue. I doubt if the Russian
could see my point. They were convinced, because of thei
Marxist indoctrination, that once a Communist revolutio
had happened, a single party met the needs of the 'liberated
masses. The only freedom necessary for the people was th
freedom to choose between people, all of whom held th
same point of view. I remember arguing with a Communis
at Cambridge on this point. He gave an illuminating
illustration:

'If you had to elect a new Archbishop of Canterbury,' h
said, 'you would make a short list of suitable members of th
Church of England. You would not put on the list Non-
conformists, Roman Catholics or atheists.'

'Quite so,' I replied. 'But the assumption is that the elector
are convinced Anglicans and are all agreed that it is desirabl
to fill the vacant archbishopric. It would be quite a differen
matter if the people of England were compelled as a natior
to take part in the election, whether or not they are Christian
and Anglicans.'

And that is the point of issue between West and East.
have no objection to the single list of Communist candidates
so long as it is meant for Communist voters. By all means le
the Party supply their adherents with suitable names, but le
other parties put forward their lists for the benefit of those
who think there is a better way than Marxism for running the
country. But that, of course, is precisely why people like
myself are the despair of the Communists. A Marxist ordering
of society is not a matter for argument; it is an economic
necessity demanded by the dialectical movement in history.
Once the clock has chimed noon it's no use discussing how
we shall spend the morning hours. They've gone, never to

eturn. Party government was necessary when Russia was split into classes and it was appropriate that the electorate should argue. But those days are over. A new society has appeared and the electorate does not wish to argue about a situation which no longer exists.

3. The place of propaganda in elections. I never know how much political propaganda achieves in this country. So much that is obviously bogus is put out from all sides that most of us take little notice. During a campaign there are so many claims and counter-claims, so many ridiculous misrepresentations and half-truths, we are content to leave it to the rival candidates to cancel one another out. And, if my parish is typical, what 'Our Dad' says counts for more than all the newspaper headlines and radio speeches put together.

It is, of course, a different matter when the propaganda comes from only one source. And people in this country may well ask—if there are no rival parties, why should a Government bother about propaganda? They are bound to win the next election whatever happens, so why trouble to convince the voters? It is not as simple as that. The Russian Communists are compelled by their Marxist doctrines to believe that, with the overthrow of the Tsarist régime, the classless society came into existence. It's difficult for us fully to appreciate this claim. Even if we could accept it as a fact, which most of us don't, we would not regard it as of catastrophic importance. But to the Marxist the world made a fresh start in 1917; in fact his philosophy tells him that everything that happened before that date belongs to pre-history. The real history of the human race started when the dialectical movement in society ended the tension between the *bourgeoisie* and the proletariat and, under the leadership of Lenin, the glorious community of justice and brotherhood came to birth. For this reason Marxists look upon their Government as the guardians of the second Eden. Their every action has one end in view—the furtherance of the golden age and endless bliss for Soviet Adam. The converse is believed with equal conviction. Any criticism of the Government and any person found blameworthy in the eyes of the Soviet Creator is guilty of wanting to restore the jungle conditions of pre history and of wrecking the golden age. The conspirators and saboteurs, when discovered in their nakedness, are led forth from Eden, which is guarded by the watchful spirits of the M.K.V.D., and are sent to work by the sweat of their brow on the soil of Siberia.

Once the myth is accepted, propaganda is inevitable. News is faked, history books are doctored and facts distorted. The newspapers and radio are used, not primarily for the expression of facts, but for the bolstering up of Eden.

The valuation of Trotsky by Soviet historians is interesting. Lenin, commenting upon his generalship, remarked: 'Show me another man who could have practically created a model army in a year and won the respect of military specialists as well.' But when the official *History of the Communist Party of the Soviet Union* was written some years later, Lenin was dead and Trotsky had been cast out of Eden. No longer is he a genius, but a military nincompoop whose incompetence nearly brought defeat to the armies of the Revolution. We can smile and wonder how intelligent people can swallow such rubbish, but once the myth has been accepted there is no escape. Stalin had become the Soviet Creator and Trotsky, by the mere fact of criticizing him, was guilty of eating the forbidden fruit.

I had considerable fun with my guides by asking them seemingly innocent questions about the early Bolshevik leaders, most of whom were murdered by Stalin. I suggested I might be shown their portraits or look at their books. I was invariably told that nothing was known about them except they were enemies of the people and tried to restore capitalism. But, and this is where I saw propaganda doing its work, I was immediately reminded that it was due to the devotion of a watchful Government that the glorious workers' paradise was unimpaired.

Lysenko afforded some problems for my friends as the official line showed signs of change. Marxist philosophy, as propounded by Stalin, had demanded an approach to genetics that was rejected by reputable scientists throughout the world. It was not unlike the situation that existed between the Pope and Galileo. Catholic dogma insisted upon a particular geographical approach to earth, heaven and hell and anybody who suggested an alternative was guilty of upsetting a whole scheme of salvation. So the propaganda machine set about the disposal of Galileo. With Lysenko it was the other way on. The value of his theory to the Marxist designer is that, if correct, it means that ultimately human beings can be produced with environmental characteristics that will overcome hereditary weaknesses. Unfortunately the evidence does not justify Lysenko in his suppositions, but the propaganda machine has compelled the Academy of Sciences to uphold him. What will happen now, it's difficult to say. Lysenko may be cast forth as a fallen angel from the Soviet Eden; even so, the Academy of Sciences has been reduced to the rank of State magician.

I discussed the point with my guide in Red Square while we were watching the changing of the guard outside Lenin's tomb.

'The real difference between the two of us,' I said, 'is that you make a great deal of fuss and bother about the corpses of Lenin and Stalin, because you believe that human experience is limited to this world. For that reason you think you have got to produce the perfect man and the perfect society on this side of the grave. Lenin and Stalin were ordinary mortals with some outstanding gifts and, from my point of view, some outstanding vices, but you have deified them because you want to present them to the Russian public as the archetypes of Soviet Man. To me this mausoleum is a piece of specious propaganda.'

'But don't you look forward to the time when mankind will be perfect? In the Soviet Union we have created the conditions which make perfection a possibility. We are a long way from our goal, but we are on the road.'

'I certainly hope that men will achieve perfection, but I don't believe it will be on this side of the grave. This doesn't mean that I turn my back upon this world. By all means let's improve outward conditions and let's make use of science, education and psychiatry to develop character; but every generation has to grapple with the perversity of the human heart. It's what we Christians call "original sin"; but I can't expect you to understand that!'

'I'm not sure what you mean by the perversity of the heart, but I certainly don't believe there's anything basically wrong with human nature.'

'In which case it's odd how frequently your great men need to be purged.'

'That's because they did not assess a situation correctly, or were selfish and out for personal power and gain.'

'Precisely. And do you really think that even if the whole world accepts the Marxist creed it will be any different in a thousand years? Won't men still assess situations wrongly, be selfish and out for personal power and gain?'

'You are wrong. The science of genetics has proved that given the right conditions you can achieve the desired product. That has been the contribution of Comrade Lysenko. You in the West still think in terms of Darwinian evolution, but our explanation is more radical.'

'And what is that?'

'The solar system came from cold dust clouds which turned with increasing speed. In course of time the clouds separated themselves. The main part became the sun, the others became different parts of the solar system. For a long time everything was non-organic, but with the passage of time there was a transformation from non-organic to organic. And that led to life as we know it. But that isn't all. A leading woman scientist in the Soviet Union, Comrade Lepeshinskaya, has been successful in transforming the non-organic into the organic. She created organic life from non-organic matter.'

'I am, of course, in no position to argue these points with you because, apart from my own lack of knowledge, you cannot produce the evidence to convince me of the truth of Lepeshinskaya's claim. But I presume that what you are trying to tell me is that one day the perfect society will be peopled with the products from test tubes?'

'I would not put it as crudely as that. But we know that science education and the right environment will overcome human limitations.'

'Man, in his foolishness and pride, has always thought that. The expression of his thought may change, but his insufferable vanity is constant. If you were allowed to read the Bible you would learn about some ancestors of ours who thousands of years ago tried to build a tower to reach the heavens. And I don't suppose they were the first to think they could achieve perfection through their own efforts; just as you certainly won't be the last. Babel is the recurring decimal in every generation.'

'You are the victim of the capitalist system. You are persuaded to believe that things will always be bad in the hope that nobody will want to bring about improvements.'

'Nothing could be farther from the truth. I happen to be an officer in a society, the Church, which exists to alter mankind for the better. But we are under no illusions about the job. We know it's a long process; we begin in this world and we continue beyond it. What is more, the job has to be done in the heart of every human being, in every generation. When you speak of Soviet Man you suggest that standards which may apply in one generation will automatically apply in another. I deny this. Even if you succeed in producing kindly, unselfish, hard-working men this year, you will face similar problems a century hence. Even when you have got your saint, his son may well turn out to be a criminal. Meanwhile your propaganda machine states the contrary. The new world has arrived and the Soviet Union, led by a wise and benevolent Government, is peopled with the sons and daughters of the new age. Your more thoughtful citizens must wonder why your newspapers contain so many denunciations of idleness, graft and corruption. I sometimes think that Stalin saw through the whole thing and he resorted to cruelty and barbarism to keep the pieces together. In fact, to put it bluntly, in the end he probably became so desperate he went off his head. That's why I find it difficult to treat either Comrade Lysenko or this mausoleum with seriousness.'

Fortunately the Kremlin clock chimed the hour and we had to bring our conversation to an end to watch the changing of the guard before the tomb of the Soviet archetypes. After the ceremony I suggested we went to the stores in search of icecream. I thought it might help to reduce the temperature.

4. An interesting Marxist doctrine is the withering away of the State. We are told that in a non-Communist country the Government is the weapon of the ruling class to suppress the proletariat. In a Communist country the Government is a dictatorship of the proletariat to establish the new society and to uproot vestiges of the old régime. The dictatorship is temporary. When the classless society has been achieved, the apparatus of the State will wither away and there will be neither need nor scope for oppressive methods. Such an assumption depends upon a curious estimate of human nature. There is nothing in the experience of man to suggest that he will willingly surrender his privileges; on the contrary, once he has tasted power, he will cling to it. A Stalin always breeds a multitude of lesser Stalins and, within a comparatively short

time, they become a class apart, a power-seeking hierarchy. Friends of mine who have held office in municipal and national politics have told me how hard they have found it to readjust themselves after retirement or defeat. John Jones becomes Lord Mayor and, as First Citizen of a great city, he walks on red carpet for a year. He takes precedence on most occasions; he's fêted, humoured and praised; he's relieved of domestic worries and is provided with every comfort and convenience. It's just as well the statutory limit is twelve months! If a Lord Mayor were allowed to continue in office indefinitely, it is unlikely that many would voluntarily resign. They would hold on as long as possible and hope to be succeeded by their sons. And who can blame them? Most of us, if we're honest, like the plaudits of the throng and to perch on the top rung of the ladder, above the hurly-burly.

And what of the power motive? That is something Marxism has never faced. Covetousness is not the only sin. The desire to dominate over others has caused just as much havoc. Petty tryanny is to be found at every level. We encounter it in the home, the prep-school, the workshop, the farmyard, the hospital. Men love to lay down the law and to bend others to their will. Most of us prefer to boss than to be bossed. That is why we are wise in this country to have elections every five years. It is an exaggeration to say that an Englishman's basic political conviction is to vote out whatever Government happens to be in power, but there's a measure of truth in it. A long experience has shown us that men should not hold the reins of power for too long. One day Russia will come to the same conclusion.

Chapter Nine

WAR OR PEACE

'Do you think they want war?' asked the customs officer at London Airport. He was the first of dozens to put the same question to me on my return to England. I have no doubt about the answer: 'Certainly not—but their crazy doctrines may create a situation from which it will be difficult to withdraw peaceably.'

The Soviet people loathe war. They are still mourning their dead in the last war. The official figure, probably an underestimate, is seventeen million. I did not meet a person during my stay in Moscow who had not lost a relative. And the devastation was appalling. I saw the ruins of Cologne and of some of the German cities, but I am told that they give little idea of the mass destruction in Russia. Even if the Communist leaders wanted to start another conflict, it would be difficult for them to win the support of their people. Of course they might succeed if they prepared the way with skilful propaganda, but there is little sign of that. I am not suggesting that there isn't talk about the possibility of a defensive war; there's a great deal and I shall refer to it shortly. But that is different from the aggressive outbursts which poured from the lips of the Nazis. They planned a campaign of conquest; Hitler wrote about it; it was the rabble-rousing theme of all his henchmen; the country was placed upon a war economy. There's nothing like that in Russia. The people are not being urged to launch a crusade against the West. The country is certainly not on a war economy; in fact, the contrary. The standard of living is continuously rising and prices are coming down. Goering told the Germans they must have guns before butter; the Russians are getting more butter and meat, bread, sugar, and clothing. A war would wreck the Government's drive for consumer goods. And there are the new buildings, thousands of them, whole cities. If the Government were bent on war, it would not devote such a large proportion of the budget to domestic buildings, least of all in the most vulnerable areas.

In any case, given the Marxist viewpoint, a war of aggression is unnecessary. Sooner or later the capitalist countries will fall like over-ripe plums into the Soviet lap; so why risk bringing civilization down in ruins when the goal can be achieved without exploding a single bomb? It's true that Stalin's treatment of Finland and the Baltic countries may seem to contradict what I have said, but I am convinced that, deplorable though it was, it was essentially to safeguard the Soviet frontiers, as a glance at a map will quickly show.

When I told the Russians that we in the West looked upon their Government as the main threat to peace they were flabbergasted. I am sure they thought they were completely honest when they said they had no aggressive designs against anybody and disclaimed territorial ambitions.

But, alas, it's not as easy as that. The Russians are the victims of their doctrines and, almost without knowing it, they may find themselves beginning what they will sincerely imagine to be a defensive action. Two things in particular can lead to trouble; their inflammatory denunciations of the West and their conviction that the capitalist countries must unleash an imperialistic war.

If the Smiths are told incessantly that the Browns, who live next door, are worse than barbarians and are not fit to be alive, it's possible that sooner or later the Smith children will throw a stone at the window of the dreadful Browns. And if we substitute Russia and the West for the Smiths and the Browns we get some idea of the situation. And here, reader, you must be patient and grasp a Marxist doctrine. It's an implication of dialectical materialism, which we've already discussed. Marxism states categorically that a just ordering of society can only come as a result of a Communist uprising, probably necessitating civil war. It scorns the methods of parliamentary democracy and gradual change. It must be revolution, not reformism.

The immediate reaction of the tolerant Englishman is: 'Why bother? If they believe this twaddle, let them get on with it.' Unfortunately we have to bother because the consequences of this belief are as poisonous as they are dangerous. The Russian people are made to believe that their country and the satellites which have had Communist revolutions are the only countries in the world which offer hope, decency and justice to the masses. The other countries, the victims of parliamentary democracy and fascism, are heading for economic collapse. Conditions are growing steadily worse. The capitalists are wallowing in riches and the common people are reduced to squalor, misery and starvation. At this stage, reader, you will want to rub your eyes and break into laughter, but you must remember that for nearly forty years millions of Russians have had this nonsense pumped into them every day of their lives and are never allowed an opportunity to learn the truth.

I have referred to the text-book I obtained from the headmaster of school No. 315 in Moscow. It's called *English Reader for the Ninth Class*. It's on my desk as I write. We'll have a look at it because it will show you what the senior children in Soviet schools are taught about our country.

The book begins with a quotation from *Ivanhoe*. In the introduction the Soviet commentator says: 'Scott introduces Robin Hood, a beloved legendary hero of the English people. In general, the ballads about Robin Hood express the mood of the peasant masses of the fourteenth and fifteenth centuries and their deep hatred of the Church authorities and feudal lords who oppressed them. In all the ballads, Robin Hood is the hero of people without property.' Harmless enough; but in the context of the book the Soviet reader is encouraged to believe that the conditions of former centuries prevail today.

Next comes Robert Burns. 'He lived in the period of the French Revolution and was an ardent supporter of its ideas. His poetry is deeply democratic and full of criticism directed against the landlords, the priests and the Government officials. In the poem "A Man's a Man for all that" he tells of a future when all men will be equal.'

Third on the list is Byron, the revolutionary romanticist. 'In the poet's own country, the workers were being mercilessly exploited; as a result of the Industrial Revolution and of the introduction of new, perfected machinery into factories, there was mass unemployment and misery among the workers. All this aroused deep indignation in Byron. From his early youth, he displayed deep hatred of tyranny and oppression and profound sympathy for the oppressed.'

Shelley is commended with a quotation from Marx. If he had not died so young, 'he would always have been in the vanguard of socialism'. The synopsis of his life is interesting. 'When he was nineteen years old, he was expelled from Oxford University for writing a pamphlet about "The Necessity of Atheism". In all his works he criticized capitalism and defended the rights of the workers. For many years of his life Shelley thought that the ideal state of society could be achieved by a peaceful revolution and by passive resistance to tyranny. The development of the class-struggle in England and the ruthless measures taken by the reactionary English Government to suppress the workers convinced him of the futility of such a theory. In the "Song to the Men of England", Shelley calls upon the workers to take up arms in their own defence.'

Charles Dickens provides a field day. As his works are often produced as plays and films in the Soviet Union, the quotations from this book are of special interest.

'When Charles Dickens was ten years old, his father, a clerk in a London naval office, was taken to prison for debt. Little Charles, the second of eight children, had to go to work in a blacking factory where he worked from early morning till late at night. When his father came out of prison, Charles was sent to school. But at fifteen he left school to work as a clerk in a lawyer's office.

'His work as a reporter in Parliament made him acquainted with the machinations in the Government and aroused in him a deep contempt for the English parliamentary system—a contempt that lasted all his life and is reflected in many of his works, beginning with *The Pickwick Club*.

'There is much humour in Dickens's works, especially in *The Pickwick Club*. But even in this, one of his earliest works, the humour is often turned into irony and satire, which the author used as powerful weapons with which to criticize and expose various evils in English social and political life: the capitalist exploiting system of workhouses in *Oliver Twist*, the *bourgeois* so-called education in *Nicholas Nickleby*, *David Copperfield* and others, capitalist cruelty and injustice in all his works.

'In 1842 Dickens visited America and then wrote *American Notes* and *Martin Chuzzlewit*. In these two books Dickens gives a highly realistic picture of American *bourgeois* society —its hypocrisy, ignorance and greed. He shows the disgusting influence of money, and directs all the force of his satire against false American democracy, against slavery, and the corruption of the American press.'

Then come the excerpts. The first, from one point of view, is gloriously amusing. Its intention is to describe the workings and effects of parliamentary democracy. It is, of course, the Eatanswill election! And here's the introduction: 'Mr Pickwick and his friends arrive in the town of Eatanswill in time to witness an election campaign; the two contending parties are the Blues and the Buffs. Neither Mr Pickwick nor anyone else knows the difference between the Blues and the Buffs, or what they stand for. But there are political jobs which the political leaders and their friends hope to get; so that each side tries to win the victory by any means. Dickens here satirizes the two leading political parties of the England of his time, and shows his contempt for both parties. Two chief political parties exist today in England, America and other capitalist countries. Both parties equally represent the capitalist system. They are like two peas out of one pod. But the capitalist two-party system makes it easier to deceive the masses and to keep control of the Government always in the hands of one party or the other.'

The introduction to the excerpt from *David Copperfield* is on much the same lines. The schoolmasters are wicked men—'Cruel, formal, narrow-minded, hypocritical; they reflect in their methods of teaching the *bourgeois* system of so-called education.'

The second half of *English Reader for the Ninth Class* is devoted to American writers. And now the author really gets going. His criticisms of Britain are mild and gentlemanly in comparison with his philippics against our Atlantic cousins. Hell becomes a Butlin's camp when matched with the United States!

Since my return from Moscow I have referred to this book with its travesty of Western democracy on several platforms. 'Fellow-travellers' in the audience have said: 'But it's true. Dickens was depicting life in the last century. You can't blame the Soviet Union for presenting the facts to their children.' That is the sort of half-truth our Stalin-worshippers love. The intention of the book is to persuade Soviet youth that the conditions which used to prevail in Britain still prevail. Page after page is devoted to denigration. Everything in England is bad. The rich gloat over the sufferings of the poor. The masses eke out a wretched existence in appalling conditions. The authorities in Church and State are corrupt hypocrites. There is no chance of justice without a proletarian revolution. Not one line in the book suggests there has been a change for the better. Education, health services, pension schemes, housing-estates, trade union legislation, welfare provisions are completely ignored. The British way of life is not merely distorted. The picture given to the readers at no point resembles the facts. It is a falsification. But that is the book's purpose. It provides the data for the Marxist theorem. Only a Communist ordering of society, brought into being through a Communist revolution, can provide the workers of the world with the necessaries of life. It is useless to argue that the Soviet authorities should allow their children to know the facts about modern Britain because the facts make nonsense of Marxist doctrines. If Russian citizens were allowed to visit England and see for themselves they would discover a standard of living well above their own; and they would quickly realize that the standard has been achieved by the reforming methods of parliamentary democracy. The real differences between our two systems of education is that ours, although it leaves much to be desired, believes that Truth is objective; to the Soviets it is relative; facts are invented and construed to support a hypothesis.

A glaring instance of this came my way when I was visiting Moscow University. While I was waiting in the large vestibule I glanced at the bookstall. I noticed a book called *English* by M. Galinskaya. It set out to do for undergraduates what *English Reader for the Ninth Class* did for children. It was, of course, a tissue of lies. In the chapter on education Galinskaya contrasts the British system with the Soviet. He says that although all children in England are supposed to attend junior and secondary schools, many cannot go to secondary schools because their parents cannot afford the fees. But that is not all—lots never go to school. 'Even now a great many English children do not attend school because their parents have no money to buy clothes and text-books for them. In 1948, 500,000 children in England could not attend school.' As a rule I have an even temper, but now I was really angry. I summoned my guide and a member of the university staff and spoke straightly to them. Holding the book in my hand I asked: 'Who reads this?'

'The English faculty.'

'It's a pack of lies and it's an insult to my country.'

'Why?'

'Read for yourself what Galinskaya says about the British educational system—secondary education is a farce, and half a million do not go to school at all. Nothing could be farther from the truth. Education in Britain is free and everybody is compelled to go, whether they want to or not. What is more, our children go for more years than yours do and we do not work on double shifts.'

'But we know that is not true. You have to be rich to send a child to secondary school.'

'That is the sort of nonsense you poor indoctrinated dolts believe. Come to Britain and see for yourselves. Not that it would make any difference. Your Government will continue to employ puppets like Galinskaya to pour out venom and abuse against England, because you are terrified of the truth.'

My explosion took them by surprise, and for a while there was silence. They did not know how to soothe such an awkward customer. I felt sorry for them. They usually had to deal with 'fellow-travellers' who are never happier than when the Soviet Union is being lauded to the skies and their own country is being damned. They had little experience of an Englishman whose conception of truth is expressed in the Bible and not in the *Daily Worker* and who, although not a jingoist, loves his country.

But there's the difficulty. Can the Soviet authorities be persuaded to change their attitude toward the democracies? It is useless for them to claim to be 'peace-loving' when their propaganda machine is stirring up hatred and misunderstanding. I don't know the answer. If I, as a Christian, were

asked to jettison the doctrine of the incarnation or the atone-
ment, I should have to refuse because to do so would wreck
the foundations of the faith. For the Communist to admit that
progress toward a just ordering of society has been achieved
by parliamentary democracy is to dislodge the corner-stone of
Marxism. The sacred creed of Karl Marx states that without
a proletarian revolution conditions for the workers must get
worse and worse. And Karl Marx is infallible. Will the day
come when the Russians will realize that, although Marx
made a useful analysis of society as he knew it, he talked an
incredible amount of nonsense as well and in many matters
was surprisingly foolish and uninformed?

In Britain there has been an immense change in the balance
of power during the past century and capitalism has been
compelled to yield vast areas of its territory. We have had a
revolution, but it has been gradual and usually silent. What
is more, men in every party have seen the necessity for it and
the fundamental structure of the Welfare State is admitted by
all responsible politicians. The impetus has come from the
radical forces, but the conservatives have not always been
unsympathetic. Although there is an inevitable tension
between employer and employee, both sides have shown
themselves capable of working together for the good of the
community. The Soviets, of course, cannot yet see this. I
remember my guide telling me that he knew the Churchill
Government had withdrawn the few privileges given to the
hungry masses by Mr Attlee and his colleagues. 'The housing
conditions are terrible,' he said.

'In fact,' I replied, 'the conditions are infinitely better than
in the Soviet Union.'

'But your housing-estates are just shacks and the conditions
are dreadful.'

'Once again, come and see for yourself. The average house
on an estate is a great deal better than anything I've seen in
Moscow.'

Sooner or later the truth must leak out. This particular guide was an intelligent fellow. One day he will be compelled to question the propaganda. A nation can be fooled for a long time, but there's bound to be a limit. More and more Russians are going to the University and are inevitably developing critical faculties. Moreover, it is impossible to isolate a great nation from the rest of the world. Scientists, engineers, traders, doctors and authors are bound to resume normal contacts with their opposite numbers in the Western democracies and the facts will emerge. And it is not impossible that the politicians will eventually become bored with the stupidities of Marxism. A hate campaign may be tolerable for half a century, but ultimately it loses its appeal. As a young man, enthusiastic for social reform, I used to read the *Daily Worker*. For a while I accepted it as gospel. But the human spirit cannot be fed on hate and lies indefinitely and it was with a sigh of relief I returned to *The Times*, and I never see the *Daily Worker* except at the Athenaeum. I am as keen on reform as I have ever been and there are still many changes in the interests of social justice I want to see in Britain, but I prefer to rely on the methods of common sense and persuasion. I know it's a long-term policy, but better that way than an upheaval that degrades human personality and sows dragons' teeth. I suppose that one's views of the future depend in the last resort upon one's assessment of the human spirit. I remember Sir Stafford Cripps, when he was ambassador in Moscow, saying that although he found little in the situation to encourage him at the time, he believed that the crazy nightmare would pass. When we discussed this some years later he referred to the conflict between Sparta and Athens. Two different ways of treating human beings: Sparta produces quick returns, but Athens makes the greater and more lasting contribution. I have a sufficiently strong belief in the basic qualities of man to believe that Pericles will one day influence the Kremlin, providing there is still a Kremlin to influence.

So much for the folly of calling people names, of the dangers that may follow if the Smiths of the Soviet Union persist in telling their children that the Browns of the Western democracies are the scum of the earth.

The other Marxist doctrine likely to cause a war is the one that asserts that capitalism, when it begins to disintegrate, can only hope to survive if it initiates imperialistic ventures. Karl Marx argued that because capitalists cannot expand indefinitely in their own country they must snatch overseas markets. The trouble begins when groups of capitalists from different countries come into collision. According to the Communists both the great wars in this century were basically a struggle for markets. We wanted to knock out Germany from the scramble and Germany wished no rivals at all. And there is another reason. The contradictions within the capitalist system are such that the unemployed masses must either overthrow the capitalist system or they must be absorbed in the fighting services. As capitalism cannot supply them with fodder, they themselves become cannon fodder. Again, let me make it clear—although we regard this analysis as superficial and inadequate, the Communists believe it. For years the Russians have had it pumped into them that the Western democracies are bound to start an imperialistic war. And this inevitably means that the Soviet Union must be attacked. This doctrine is rammed home in the press, on the radio and on the stage.

Before setting off to Russia, Harold Wilson told me to make every effort to see the great ballerina, Oulanova. I did and I was successful. Oulanova is almost supernatural. I am fond of ballet and I've seen several ballerinas, but I've never watched anything like the performance of Oulanova. It is not often that in this life one thinks one has witnessed perfection, but this was such an occasion. If everything else about my visit had been a hopeless failure, Oulanova would have been sufficient compensation. And yet as a Westerner

WAR OR PEACE

I suppose I ought to have walked out of the Bolshoi theatre at the end of the first act as the theme of the ballet, called *Red Poppy*, was a disgraceful portrayal of the alleged imperialistic designs of the West.

The opening scene showed the Chinese coolies floundering helplessly on the stage beneath enormous burdens. From time to time officers in American uniform appeared from a gin palace with prostitutes on their arms to thrash the coolies. Their hero is Oulanova who, representing the soul of China, plays the title role. Red Poppy constantly appears to encourage and comfort the down-trodden masses, although in doing so she has to resist the blandishments of the Americans who are anxious to seduce her. Capitalism, cruelty, adultery, drunkenness and barbarism seem triumphant until a Soviet cruiser arrives and lets loose among the coolies the heralds and architects of a new civilization. The rest of the ballet depicts the conflict between the two sides and, needless to add, Red Poppy is saved from the wicked Americans and the coolies are set free. The epilogue was a ballet of red flags. It was beautiful and impressive. The audience cheered madly at the end. And so did I, as I was captivated by Oulanova. The applause lasted fifteen minutes, and she must have taken a dozen curtain calls. My Russian friend remarked: 'What a wonderful ballet! What did you think of it?'

'I thought it was tragic that the greatest ballerina in the world should prostitute her gifts in the interests of your crazy and wicked doctrines.'

'I don't know why you should feel so strongly. I know the Western soldiers used to be in British uniforms, but, as you have seen for yourself, they've changed them for American ones.'

'That isn't the point. You and your Government are continually talking about "peace-loving nations" and this ballet is doing its best to sow the seeds of bitterness, misunderstanding and war.'

'But the Americans want war. We are merely warning our people to be on the defensive.'

'Some Americans may want war, but the vast majority don't. I'm certainly not trying to defend the foreign policy of Mr Dulles, some of which is almost as bad as yours, but the idea that the American nation is ready and anxious to bring down the world in ruins is fantastic.'

We had reached the steps outside the Bolshoi theatre and my friend tried to conclude on an agreeable note by saying that at least *Red Poppy* pointed the world to a glorious future of brotherhood and equality. As he was speaking I noticed the smart chauffeur-driven limousines taking away the heads of the régime. In the streets, and it was nearly midnight, women were doing hard manual work for a pittance. How easy it is to become so indoctrinated that one can no longer distinguish between fact and phantasy! Marxist Russia is indeed a Cloud-cuckoo world.

The cinemas are used for the same purpose. During my last week in Moscow the main attraction was a film called *Silver Dust*. It was advertised in every area in the city and was to be seen at eighteen cinemas. Here's the theme: An American capitalist with the help of an escaped Nazi tried to discover a substance, silver dust, to bring death to the people on whom it is sprayed. It is, of course, to be used against the Soviet Union. The American is confronted by immense difficulties and he gets discouraged. Along comes a priest who tells him that he has just had a vision of Jesus Christ and Christ wants him to go ahead with his work. So the American and the Nazi experiment on black people who are brought, against their will, into the laboratory. They are killed off like guinea pigs at a vivisectionist's. In the end the glorious gospel of Karl Marx comes to the rescue and the wicked American plot to bring death and destruction to the Soviet Union is foiled.

My guide was a little touchy when I asked him to take me to the film. He remembered my reactions to *Red Poppy*.

'I don't think it would be convenient to see *Silver Dust* today.'

'Then we'll go tomorrow.'

'But I don't think you would like it.'

'I'm quite sure I wouldn't. All the more reason why I want to see it. I want to tell my fellow-countrymen what a "peace-loving" film is like. What is more, as a priest I am interested in the vision of my colleague.'

'You have misunderstood our intentions. We bear no ill-will against the British and American peoples. It is the Governments that are at fault.'

'If the Governments are as bad as you make them out to be, then why didn't they make a pact with Hitler and destroy the Soviet Union?'

'They did the next-best thing.'

'What do you mean?'

'Churchill delayed the second front for several years so that the Russians could be defeated. It was only when he saw we were stronger than Hitler that he allowed a small expeditionary force to cross the Channel.'

'Do you really believe that?'

'Yes. We know it's true. Britain and America played at soldiers. They didn't come onto the scene until Stalin had accomplished the defeat of the Nazis.'

'I suppose you think our casualty list was an invention, and that Coventry, London, Bristol, Plymouth, Southampton and the other cities were never bombed?'

'But you never really wanted to smash Hitler. Your main concern was to destroy the Soviet Union.'

'In that case why did we stand alone in 1940? Don't forget your wonderful Stalin was toasting Hitler and your great "peace-loving" Molotov was Ribbentrop's buddy when we had our backs to the wall. If we hadn't gone on with the fight when you were extolling the glories of Germany you would have been without an ally when the Nazis turned against you. Your death roll was terribly severe, I know; it would have been worse if we had not been prepared to die when we were alone. To me it is tragic beyond words that you can trick yourself into believing what is so manifestly untrue.'

He didn't reply. I suspect he knew he couldn't; for once the Marxist formula had failed him.

The appalling effects of the doctrine came home most vividly in my dealings with the Baptist Church. On my last Sunday in Moscow I had spent the afternoon on a tour of the countryside with the British Ambassador and Lady Hayter. When we returned to the Embassy they asked me to stay for tea, but, as it was late, I thought I had better get back to my hotel. I walked at a leisurely pace along the river, over the bridge and across Red Square. My guide, whom I was not expecting to see, was waiting for me at the entrance of the National. 'Hurry up,' he said. 'You are to preach at the Baptist Church.' I was astonished. Nothing had been said to warn me. It was already half-past five and the service was due to begin in a few minutes. We dived into a taxi and rushed through the streets of Moscow. I arrived at the church, which had a congregation of three thousand, in a breathless condition and quite unprepared to preach. I was given a delightful welcome in the vestry and introduced to the officials. After a prayer I was led to the rostrum, having warned my hosts I would have to leave within an hour. This was a sensible precaution because I knew how long Russian services could last. The service was much like its non-conformist counterpart in Britain—extempore prayers, readings from the Scriptures and several hymns. The presiding minister made a charming speech of introduction, and I found myself facing the vast audience. As each sentence had to be translated, my remarks were brief. I told the Baptists that as a Christian I was delighted to be with them and I brought with me the prayers and good wishes of believers in England. This produced a round of applause, which I found rather moving. I continued: 'Although our nationalities, traditions and systems may differ, you and I share a common experience. Christ is the Lord of our lives and through His death on the cross of Calvary we find forgiveness and peace. It is the fact of of our redemption and of our membership of the Church that bring us into one great family of love and brotherhood.' The reaction was just what one would have experienced in a Primitive Methodist church years ago: 'Amen. Hallelujah. Praise the Lord.' It is not the Anglican way, and I should find such ejaculations a trifle embarrassing in my own church, but in the Baptist Church in Moscow it seemed exactly right and I would not have had it otherwise. And then I said: 'I also speak to you as an Englishman, and I want you to know that we are solidly behind our Prime Minister in his great efforts for world peace and reconciliation. We hate war. We yearn for peace. Everybody in Britain stretches out the hand of brotherhood to the great Russian people.' This produced a tumult of applause and a few were moved to tears. The minister shook me warmly by the hand, said a prayer for my welfare, and called upon the congregation to sing the hymn 'God be with you till we meet again'. This they did with great feeling and at the last line produced their handkerchiefs and waved them enthusiastically. For a starchy Anglican it was a somewhat difficult situation, but I asked the minister if I might express my gratitude by giving the blessing. As soon as I raised my right hand for the purpose, the congregation replied with a further vigorous waving of handkerchiefs. As I've already suggested, it was not quite in keeping with the traditions and atmosphere of the Church of England, but I was deeply impressed by the kindliness, sincerity and spontaneity of the people. It was a privilege to be accepted in such a fashion by one's brother Christians. During the singing of the next hymn the minister led me back to the vestry to pick up my hat and coat. 'We should like to have a personal discussion with you,' he said. 'Will you come back tomorrow evening?' I gratefully accepted.

Monday's meeting with the four senior officials of the Baptist Church was interesting and disturbing. For half an hour we discussed theology. The Russians, who knew little or nothing of Western scholarship, were distressed to learn that the Churches in Britain did not, as a rule, accept the literal inspiration of the Scriptures. They asked my views on evolution, Jonah and the whale, the resurrection of the body and the creeds and they told me I was heretical. 'You are as bad as the Marxists,' said the chairman with a laugh. My guide, who acted as interpreter, was intrigued. He had thoroughly enjoyed his consignment on the previous evening. He had never been to church in his life and he suddenly found himself standing on a rostrum translating my sermon. 'I never thought such a thing could happen to me,' he remarked as we sat in the taxi. And now he had to deal with the niceties of Anglican theology. It was strange ground, but he admitted that he had no idea that any Church tried to interpret the creeds in the light of modern knowledge. It's a pity that the Orthodox and Evangelical Churches in the Soviet Union are so rigid in their approach to doctrine and have such little sympathy for the scientific mind. I am not a disciple of the late Bishop Barnes of Birmingham, but the average Anglican would be more at home with him than with the scriptural literalist in Russia.

Next we discussed the World Council of Churches. This was delicate ground. For some years the leading denominations have been in the habit of sending representatives to a world assembly. The Russian Churches have absented themselves, to the regret of the others. I was anxious to find out whether the Baptists would reconsider their attitude, though I knew the ultimate decision rested with the Soviet Government.

'We hope you will join us at the next assembly of the World Council of Churches,' I said.

'It's difficult for us. The World Council is an instrument

for American imperialism and anti-Soviet propaganda,' replied the chairman.

'That really is not the case. The Churches meet to discuss matters of mutual interest. It is not a political organization.'

'But Mr Foster Dulles has played a leading part in it.'

'I hold no brief for Mr Dulles; in fact I think some of his views are appalling, but when he addressed the assembly some years ago he did so as a member of a Church and not as an American politician. What is more, there is freedom of speech. If you had been present you could have put forward your point of view.'

'We are considering the matter and perhaps we may attend the next assembly. But we shall need a lot of convincing that the World Council is not part of the capitalist machine.'

'That's up to you. It's no good blaming the Council for being weighted with capitalists if the non-capitalists absent themselves. All the same I think it's a great pity if we think of the World Council of Churches in these terms. The economic system of a country is not our concern unless it deprives people of the necessities of life.'

At this stage one of my hosts made me a present of a book. I had noticed it on a table at my side and I had feared it was meant for me. The Patriarch had already given me a copy but, being an astute diplomatist, he had made no comment.

The book, and I have it on my desk as I write, is a verbatim account of a conference 'in the defence of peace' held at Zagorsk monastery in 1952. It is published by the Moscow Patriarchate and runs to nearly three hundred pages.

The conference was summoned by Patriarch Alexis and representatives came from all the Churches in the Communist countries. Moslems, Buddhists and Jews also attended.

It's worth quoting from the speeches of these religious 'peace lovers', because they show how widespread is the influence of Marxist doctrine.

Here is the Metropolitan Nicholas, a senior bishop of the

Russian Orthodox Church: 'When the American cannibals resorted to bacteriological war against the Korean and Chinese people, our Church issued an angry protest. These designs are prompted by such a hatred of mankind, by such malice, as has not been witnessed since the world was created. The Soviet Union towers like an impregnable citadel of Peace above the murky waves of a stormy ocean. Glory to the great Stalin.'

Archbishop Flavian of Moscow: 'At the present time, the American invaders, trampling upon all that is holy in the soul of man, are committing horrible deeds by using against the peaceful population of Korea chemical weapons, poisoning peaceful people with lethal gases and infecting by bacteriological means the population with plague, cholera, typhus and other diseases.'

His Holiness, Melkhisedek Catholicos—Patriarch of All Georgia: 'The banner of peace has been raised by the glorious son of the Georgian people, the great Stalin. The Georgian people love him and follow him, the standard-bearer of peace. The great Stalin calls to struggle for peace, and the entire Soviet people follow him. The Georgian Church has prayed for his health and long years of life and will devote all her efforts to the fight for peace. Long live the standard-bearer of peace, the great Stalin! Long live the glorious son of our people—the great Stalin!'

Nikolai Tikhonov, President of the Soviet Peace Committee: 'We all know and profoundly believe that, notwithstanding the intrigues of the warmakers, the "crusades" they are launching, notwithstanding the diverse machinations of the warmakers, the great cause of Peace will triumph because the great army of Peace supporters grows stronger every day, every hour; because this army unites all upright men and women of the globe; because it is led by the great champion of Peace, the friend of all progressive humanity, the greatest man of our time—Joseph Vissarionovich Stalin!'

Metropolitan Sebastian of the Rumanian Orthodox Church: 'Our people are filled with profound indignation whenever they hear of the threat of war, whenever they hear of instances of the criminal imperialists inciting and preparing a new world war. The ardent love cherished by our people for the Soviet Union and its leader, the genius J. V. Stalin, is all the greater since they see today in their liberators of yesterday the defenders of their right to life.'

Ivan Manayenko, President of the Spiritual-Christians: 'The aggressors of the U.S.A. and Great Britain are transforming cities and settlements into fire-swept wastes and deserts and are annihilating the industrious population of Korea. They are infecting healthy people in Korea and China with death-dealing germs. It is with tears of fervent feeling that the Spiritual-Christians offer their ardent prayers for Joseph Vissarionovich Stalin, the great leader of nations, the bearer of the banner of peace, and from the bottom of their hearts they wish him long life to the joy of the whole of progressive mankind.'

Khiyaletdinov, President of the Moslem Council for the European part of the U.S.S.R. and Siberia: 'On behalf of the Moslems of the European part of the U.S.S.R. and Siberia, and on my own behalf, I demand that an immediate end be put to the barbarous deeds of the imperialists threatening to spread terrible epidemical, lethal diseases in the countries of north-east Asia. I protest against their crimes and call upon the Moslems of the world, in the interests of mankind, to force the American cannibals to discontinue the use of bacteriological and chemical weapons and prevent the utilization of atomic energy for the wholesale extermination of people! Long live the friend of the working people of the whole world and champion of Peace, the wise Stalin! Amen!'

Archbishop Jaan Kiivit of the Estonian Lutheran Church: 'The American and British imperialists are making fiendish use of the Christian faith as a screen for their strivings to enslave the peoples and to seize the territories of other States. We protest at the Christian faith being turned into a screen for foul crimes. We protest at the neo-fascist theoreticians justifying the use of inter-continental rockets, the bacteriological weapons, death-dealing gases, the employment of atomic and hydrogen bombs. The war criminals shall have to bear the responsibility for this before an international court. Let us do everything possible to halt the fiendish designs of the warmongers.'

Solomon Shliffer, Rabbi of the Moscow Synagogue: 'Now that the warmongers are preparing a new slaughter, planning to deprive us of the freedoms gained and to destroy them, we Jews, like one man, must enter the ranks of fighters for peace. Bacteriological warfare is a heinous outrage, a monstrous crime against humanity! Can the prayer of such bigots and hypocrites be acceptable to God? May there be Peace throughout the world as wish all men of goodwill headed by the bulwark of Peace, the great Soviet Union, which is led by the standard-bearer of Peace, the leader and inspirer of peace-loving peoples, the great Stalin! Amen!'

Ali Zade, President of the Moslem Council for Trans-caucasia: 'Bloodthirsty American imperialism, American bankers and industrialists, losing all conscience and semblance of human beings, have embarked on the path of shameless violation of the laws of God and man. They are planning to plunge mankind into the abyss of a new bloody war. Gripped by wild ideas of world dominion, they are hatching vile schemes for subjugating the peoples and turning free men into their slaves. To accompany their bloodthirsty plans the American aggressors have now begun using the bacteriological weapon against free peoples. Lacking even the elementary human feelings, they have embarked on the wholesale destruction of people by means of deadly microbes. With this weapon they wish to annihilate the populations of entire towns and villages. Down with the warmakers! Victory to

Peace! Long live the wisest man, the torch of peace—Stalin!'

Gabzhi Lobsan-Nima, President of the Central Buddhist Council of the U.S.S.R.: 'Woe to the warmongers if, in their blindness and fury, they plunge the world into the abyss of a new cataclysm! Humanity's formidable sword will fall on their heads. They shall not escape hell and retribution, and their names shall be loathed and execrated till the end of time. Long live the great Stalin, standard-bearer of Peace.'

Toward the end of the book is a message from the Dean of Canterbury who was distressed because his official duties did not permit him to attend the Peace Conference. As I've already said, the Patriarch had given me the book, but had wisely made no comment. I suspect he knew exactly how much value ought to be attached to the so-called Peace Movement. His own contribution was a masterpiece of ecclesiastical statesmanship, combined with real charity. Alexis is a great man and a great Christian, with an extremely difficult course to steer. I don't suppose he is ever fooled.

When my Baptist friends passed me their copy, I politely waved it aside, telling them that the Patriarch had forestalled them. I tried to turn the conversation into other channels, but it was useless. 'What do you think of the book?' asked the Chairman.

'I prefer not to discuss it.'

'But we want to know.'

'Gentlemen, you put me into an embarrassing position. I am here as your guest, and I would prefer not to discuss a matter that is bound to be painful to my hosts.'

'We respect your sincerity and it is important we should know your reaction.'

'If you insist, I will speak frankly.'

'Go ahead. Be as outspoken as you care.'

'I will tackle it from two levels—as an Englishman, then as a fellow-Christian. How do you expect me, as an Englishman, to be anything but disgusted with such an unjust and malicious attack upon my country? You say your object is peace, but nearly every speech at the conference is calculated to stir up bad blood between our nations. In fact, if you had set out to sow the seeds of war, you could not have done the job more efficiently.'

'But we were compelled to denounce bacteriological warfare.'

'What proof have you that we used it? I do not for one moment believe that we did.'

'The Dean of Canterbury is convinced that you are guilty, and he is a leading Churchman.'

'The Dean of Canterbury is taken seriously by nobody but himself.'

'We do not say that the British peoples are to blame; it is your Churchill Government.'

'I'm afraid you are talking to the wrong man. I am no lover of the Churchill Government. I am a Socialist; I voted against the Conservatives at the last election; I shall certainly vote against them next time. But in this matter there is no difference whatever between us. Churchill speaks for all of us. When you attack him you attack the whole British nation. And no matter how much some of us may differ from Churchill in many respects, nobody can deny his ardent desire for peace. To bring about an understanding with the Soviet Union is his major concern, in spite of the exasperating provocations of the Kremlin.'

'What about the Americans? The British may want peace, but you are the servants of the United States. You allow them to have air bases on your territory. You help them to encircle the Soviet Union. Their leaders cry out for war against us. They want to enslave the backward countries for imperialistic reasons.'

'It is not for me to answer for the Americans. You had better direct your questions to Mr Bohlen.'

'But you must have some views?'

'I have. There's much in American foreign policy I dislike. A lot of it is misguided and foolish. I deplore the neurotic witch-hunt. In fact the trouble with both of you is that you haven't grown up. When Russia and America behave like adults it will be easier for all of us to work together. But don't forget that America is a democracy and, although extreme things are said and done, there are other points of view. And don't forget that America did a lot to defeat Hitler and has made a noble contribution toward the reconstruction of devastated Europe. It's a great pity you are not allowed to talk to the Ambassador, Mr Bohlen. In him you have a great representative of a great country.'

'And now, Canon Stockwood, what have you to say to us as a Christian?'

'I don't know where to begin. The book suggests that we have no point of contact. If I understand the Scriptures aright, we are pledged to use the weapons of love, truth and understanding. But those qualities seem to be entirely absent. You refer to us as "war-mongers", "cannibals", "neo-fascists", "criminals", "beasts". Can you imagine Our Lord Jesus Christ soiling his lips with such words?'

'We see your point, but perhaps you don't appreciate the intensity of our feelings?'

'I realize you believe what your Government tells you about us. That is the terrible tragedy of your Marxist propaganda. You have surrendered your critical faculty. But even so, that does not excuse the lamentable lack of Christian charity in your utterances.'

'You, in Britain, have strange and untrue ideas about us, and some of your leaders say cruel and bitter things.'

'Perhaps so. But there's a difference between a politician making a vitriolic speech and an ecclesiastic. Can you imagine the Archbishop of Canterbury describing you as "cannibals" and "beasts"? Has any bishop or nonconformist leader made a public declaration that begins to resemble what your ecclesiastics said at Zagorsk?'

'We admit that so far as we are aware the Archbishop of Canterbury always speaks with charity.'

'Well, my friends, it has pained me to speak so frankly, but you insisted that I should. I can only hope that you will think more kindly of us in the future. You say you want peace; so do we. We hate war as much as you do. Even more important, you and I believe that the only way to true peace is the way of Jesus Christ.'

'We are indebted to you, Canon Stockwood, for your honest expression of opinion.'

I suggested we should stand and say together the Lord's Prayer. We did. They asked me to pronounce the blessing. I did. 'The Peace of God, which passeth all understanding, keep your hearts and minds in the knowledge and love of God . . . the Father, the Son, and the Holy Ghost . . . Amen.'

I have given this full account of my visit to the Baptists because it shows the nature and extent of the misunderstanding between East and West. Marxist indoctrination has done its work. For years the population has heard only one point of view. The Russians are convinced that the so-called capitalist powers are trying to save themselves from economic collapse by launching an imperialistic war against the Soviet Union. Do the men of the Kremlin really believe this? I imagine the answer is 'yes' and 'no'. They are schizophrenic. When they live in their Marxist dream world they swallow their own propaganda; when they deal empirically with existing situations they know that theories and realities do not coincide. One can only hope that as the Soviet Union becomes more sure of itself its Government will realize the futility and danger of the Marxist diagnosis of the intentions of non-Communist countries. Britain has a long history and it took us many centuries to become a liberal democracy. The Soviet régime is still in its infancy and it has the touchiness, the limitations and the vulgarities of the *arriviste*. Time will have its effect. It usually mellows and modifies. But it remains to be seen whether during the interval we in the West can be sufficiently patient and wise to prevent an explosion. It's never easy to deal with a growing boy, especially when he's the victim of hallucinations, but we must try!

My visit was drawing to a close. Perhaps it was just as well. I felt that Intourist was becoming a little frustrated. They had tried to impress me with the grandeur of the Soviet experiment, but I had been awkward. I readily admired the great advances toward social justice and I was thrilled with the determination to build for the future. An immense amount that is worth while has been achieved in an astonishingly short time and there is no doubt that the standard of living is rapidly rising. Whatever may be said against Marxism, let us admit that for the majority life is a deal happier and more comfortable than it used to be. But I have a critical mind. I am always averse to propaganda and I am profoundly suspicious of political lines. If I had been prepared to swallow the workers' paradise, hook, line and sinker, I would have availed myself of a Communist-sponsored invitation to visit the Soviet Union. But this I had always refused to do. I was determined to see things for myself and to be beholden to nobody.

On my last evening I gave a small party in my rooms to the British and American Ambassadors. They had been more than kind to me and it had been a privilege to take services for their staffs. They never tried to influence my judgement, but they invariably supplied me with the information for which I asked. The hotel authorities did us proudly. I told the manager there would not be more than half a dozen, but there was sufficient caviare, salmon, fruit and champagne for twenty.

My passport, which had been taken from me on my arrival, had not been returned. I asked Mr Rogov repeatedly for it.

As I was due to leave at midnight I said to Sir William Hayter: 'You mustn't leave this hotel till I've got my papers!' Eventually he came with me to the office and the documents were handed over.

When I reached the airport we had the inevitable delay. I tried to sleep in a chair, but I couldn't get comfortable. It was six o'clock before we left and there was a slight covering of snow on the ground. At Prague I lunched with Mr and Mrs Beith of the British Embassy, but not before I had had another argument with the officials at the airport. They seemed genuinely interested in my reactions and tried to convince me that Czechoslovakia's version of Communism was better than Moscow's.

And so to Amsterdam and London. As I lay in bed in my club I thought of the many kindly courteous Russians I had met, and I began to re-live the past few weeks, wondering wherein lay the essential difference between our two countries. I pictured myself back in Red Square arguing with my guide outside Lenin's tomb. The picture became confused. It was midnight. A clock was striking. I unconsciously expected to hear the chimes of the Kremlin to which I had become accustomed. It was Big Ben.

26